AN OLD-FASHIONED

Christmas

GIFTS TO MAKE FOR FAMILY & FRIENDS

AN OLD-FASHIONED
Christmas
GIFTS TO MAKE FOR FAMILY & FRIENDS

Diana Mansour

Sedgewood® Press
New York

Published by Sedgewood ® Press

For Sedgewood ® Press
Director: Elizabeth P. Rice
Production Manager: Bill Rose

Produced for Sedgewood ® Press by
Marshall Cavendish Books Limited
58 Old Compton Street
London W1V 5PA

For Marshall Cavendish
House Editor: Dorothea Hall
Editor: Diana Mansour
Art Editor: Caroline Dewing
Production: Craig Chubb
Stylist: Kay McGlone

First printing 1988

© Marshall Cavendish Limited 1988

Distributed by Meredith Corporation

ISBN 0-696-02302-4

Library of Congress Catalog Number 87-060945

Printed in the United States of America

Contents

Introduction

Thou day of happy sound and mirth
That long wi' childish memory stays
How blest around the cottage hearth
I met thee in my boyish days . . .

from *The Shepherd's Calendar,* 1827,
by John Clare

Christmas is traditionally a time for laughter, for reconciling old differences, for parties and presents, and above all a time for sheer enjoyment of life, an oasis of exuberance in the desert of winter. Nowadays, unfortunately, it can also be a time of harassment, of spending more money than we can afford on things that we don't really want, of senseless competition and increasingly frayed tempers as the day itself draws near.

However much we may wish to preserve the Christmas message of peace and goodwill to all men, there is a tendency to become trapped in a commercialized parody of the old Christmas traditions – pagan and Christian alike – and to spend endlessly, not only on presents, but on all the other accessories, such as wreaths, tree decorations, cards, wrapping paper, Christmas napkins and place mats, and stockings. Yet Christmas is still there to be enjoyed, and most of us have an inner picture of our own ideal Christmas, influenced by happy childhood memories and pictures from storybooks, in which the decorations and presents remain but the commercial element is removed.

This book offers an escape route away from the over-commercialized twentieth-century Christmas and shows how easy, and how much more enjoyable, it is to make your own decorations and small gifts, cards and wrapping paper, stockings and place mats. With a little care and thought, the end results can be every bit as attractive and just as beautifully co-ordinated as the goods offered in the stores, but you will feel a far greater satisfaction when you have made them yourself.

However commercialized Christmas becomes, children will still enjoy the day itself, but it is the mad rush prior to the festive season that can easily become so joyless. In the last century, each household would be a hive of activity during the days before Christmas as everyone, children just as much as grown-ups, made little trinkets and boxes to hang from the tree, prepared small gifts for relatives and special friends, gathered greenery and wove it into wreaths and garlands, and generally participated to the full in the fun and excitement of preparing for the event. Much of this enjoyment, and the resulting sense of achievement, are lost if all the goods are bought ready-made.

The different chapters of this book contain a treasury of Christmas designs. A few, such as the knitted stockings, require specific skills, but the majority could be made by a complete beginner to the crafts involved, and many could be used as family projects, with children joining in the fun. Some items, such as the embroidered card, would take a little time to produce and are likely to be reserved for favored friends and relatives, but others can be made so quickly that you will wonder why you ever bothered to buy them in previous years. So try out some of the designs shown here, and experience some of the pleasures of an old-fashioned Christmas.

CHAPTER 1

Deck the halls

For so many of us, the transformation brought about by Christmas decorations is an essential part of the festive scene. Everything connected with it, from gathering bunches of evergreens to the spraying and painting and binding, and then the final moment when you stand back to admire the effect, is unforgettable fun. Traditionally the gathering of the greenery and its hanging take place just before Christmas, but a little forward planning can make an enormous difference to the finished effect. Think of Christmas before pruning any evergreen trees and shrubs in your yard. Gather and store nuts and pine cones in the late autumn, and keep cuttings of lavender, rosemary and thyme to be included in decorations. The following chapter contains many traditional evergreen decorations – including two wreaths, a swag and a garland – that are guaranteed to create that special Christmas atmosphere. In addition, there are some charming and unusual decorations, ranging from a children's candy wreath and a hanging wreath made from dried grasses and pine cones, to three-dimensional gold stars with streamers.

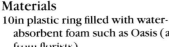

Materials

10in plastic ring filled with water-
    absorbent foam such as Oasis (available
    from florists)
Short pieces of holly, variegated holly,
    cypress, yew and pine
White straw flowers
Dried poppy seed heads
Cow parsley seed heads
Pine cones
Florist's artificial holly berries (if the holly
    has no real berries)
Gold spray
Red poster paint
2yd of 1in-wide ribbon
Floral wire, #18 gauge

Door wreath

These days many people buy their door wreaths ready-made, but in fact they are so easy to make and so rewarding that it is a shame not to give yourself the pleasure and satisfaction of making your own. Provided you carefully select the most perfect sprigs of greenery and decide in advance whether you intend to produce a wreath highlighted with gold or silver, or one that displays the traditional but always effective contrast of bright red and deep green, there is no reason why your wreath should not look every bit as good as any that a florist might produce. Bear in mind the color of your own front door: it may be that a different color scheme from the one suggested here would integrate better with the colors of your house. The wreath described here is only an example, illustrating the basic construction of a wreath, and you will almost certainly find that you are adding your own individual touches.

Preparation

Leave the ring to soak in water, so that the Oasis absorbs as much as possible, while you prepare the seed heads and pine cones.

The seeds and flowers included in this wreath are only suggestions: others, such as the silvery, rounded seed pods of honesty, may be more readily available to you and would be equally suitable.

If you are using cow-parsley seeds, spray them with gold and leave them on newspaper to dry. Also spray some of your pine cones with gold. Paint others with red poster paint.

If the seed heads are to be used in small clusters, cut 8in lengths of floral wire to bind them together. If they are to be used individually you will still find it easier to cut the stems and bind them with lengths of wire. The pine cones should be wired in a similar way: cut an 8in length of wire and

wrap the center of the wire around the lowest layer of pine petals; bring the ends together under the cone and twist them together.

Fix a length of wire through and around the ring and shape it into a small circle at the back to make a hanger.

Making the wreath

It is best to work with the wreath in place on the door. If you do not have a door knocker at a suitable height, you will have to hang the wreath on a small nail.

Start by inserting short pieces of cypress and yew around the outer

edge of the circle until the outer frame is well covered. Next, insert small pine sprigs around the inner circle, making sure that you keep the center well shaped.

Place the cones in position pushing the lengths of floral wire firmly into the Oasis. Use gold cones at the base, then place red ones around the circle and put clusters of berries at the top.

The next stage is to fill in all the remaining areas with a well-balanced mixture of variegated and green holly.

Step back frequently and take a look to make sure that the effect is balanced. When the wreath is well covered, add the seed heads, straw flowers and artificial berries, if needed. Finish by cutting the ribbon into two equal lengths and making a large double bow to pin at the base of the circle.

From time to time you'll need to take the wreath down and lay it on the ground so that you can replenish the Oasis with water.

Evergreen swag

An evergreen swag to hang on a door or to decorate a wall or an archway is one of the simplest – and prettiest – of seasonal designs, and because it is so very simple and uncluttered it can have a sophistication that more complicated arrangements sometimes lack. These little swags are so quick to make that you can easily substitute fresh greenery if the first sprigs start to look dry and unattractive before Christmas is over.

Preparation

If you are using spray paint, lightly spray the twigs on one side and lay them out on newspaper. When they have dried, turn them over and spray the other side of each twig.

Attach a length of floral wire to each nut and cone (see page 12), ready to bind them to the stems. Prepare the ornaments in the same way, threading a length of wire through the loop at the back of each one.

Making the swag

When all the stems have been prepared, lay them on your table or work surface. Place the longest and widest ones in position first, in the form of a shallow fan, and arrange the other stems over them, taking care to alternate the colors and textures.

When you are happy with the arrangement, bind the stems firmly together with wire. If you have too many bare stems gathered at one end you can cover these with a few shorter pieces of foliage.

Twist the wired nuts and cones securely around the stems, then do the same with the ornaments, first inserting short lengths of wire through the loops of each ornament and twisting firmly to hold.

If the swag is to hang indoors, it may not be necessary to wire the nuts in place. Push a piece of reusable adhesive clay (such as Blu-tack) or a piece of mount tape on one side and it can then be pressed firmly to a twig (see above).

Take a short length of ribbon and tie it around the stems in a bow, with short tails. Repeat this with the second length of ribbon, leaving long tails of ribbon to trail down. Trim the ends neatly into inverted arrows.

Attach a length of wire to the back of the swag and use this to hang it from the door.

Materials

A selection of evergreens such as pine (you can use pieces cut off the Christmas tree), ivy trails, laurel, bay, cypress and holly, and some well shaped twigs such as apple (these should be green wood, not dried twigs, which might snap)

Cones, nuts and small Christmas tree ornaments to decorate the stems

Fine wire to bind the stems

Floral wire, #18 gauge, to attach the nuts and cones

Gold or silver spray paint (optional)

1½yd of 1¼in-wide ribbon

Materials

10in plastic ring filled with water-absorbent foam such as Oasis (available from florists – this makes two horseshoes)

Short pieces of evergreens, such as yew, cypress, pine, holly and ivy

A few pine cones and glossy chestnuts

30 florist's artificial holly berries (if the holly has no real berries)

1yd of 1½in-wide florist's ribbon

1¼yd of narrow ribbon or gold cording (if wreath is to hang with ends upward)

Floral wire, #18 gauge

Horseshoe wreath

Here's a traditional welcome with a difference – a lucky horseshoe of bright and shiny evergreens to hang on the door. For added luck, make sure that it contains plenty of holly, traditionally supposed to be hateful to witches. Another tradition was that if the first holly brought indoors at Christmas time was prickly, then the man would have the mastery for the coming year; conversely, if it was smooth then the woman would rule: but perhaps Christmas is not the time to be thinking of disputes, even the battle of the sexes. Depending on the position of your door knocker, either the horseshoe can hang as shown in the picture, or you can fix lengths of ribbon or gold cording to the sides and suspend it from these, so that the wreath hangs with the two ends pointing upward, in the traditional manner.

Making the wreath

Start by cutting the Oasis-filled ring in half. Use one half and set the other to one side to make a second horseshoe or a table decoration. (It can be used to make a pretty semicircular frame of

greenery to go around a Christmas candle.)

Soak the semicircle of Oasis that is to be used for the horseshoe. Start inserting the evergreen sprigs, working from the center out to one end and then out to the other. To make sure that you have a balanced effect, it is a help if you first divide the greenery into two evenly mixed bunches. Alternate smooth and shiny foliage and spiky stems as you work. Press longer stems into the two cut edges so that the design tapers away neatly.

When you have finished inserting the greenery, wire the pine cones and nuts (see page 12) and press these in randomly but evenly around the wreath. Now twist artificial holly berries around the stems, if needed.

Form the florist's ribbon into a bow and thread a length of floral wire through the back of the loop. Press the wire into the Oasis at the center of the wreath. If the horseshoe is to hang with its ends upward (traditionally believed to hold in good luck) cut the ribbon into three equal lengths and form three bows with shorter tails – one for the center, one positioned about a third of the way up one side and one placed closer to the top at the other side.

If the wreath is to hang pointing downward, take a length of floral wire and wind it around the wreath at the central point, making sure that the wire is hidden by foliage and the bow. At the back of the wreath, twist the wires together and then form them into a loop for hanging (as shown on page 12).

If the wreath is to hang with the ends pointing upward, take two lengths of floral wire and wind one around each end of the wreath, making small loops at the back, as described above. Cut the narrow ribbon or gold cording into two lengths and thread one end of each through a loop; tie, then tie the other ends in a bow at the hanging point.

Materials

Thick sash cord, cut to length as needed (see directions)

Approximately 1lb of sphagnum moss (available from florists)

Fine wire for binding

Short pieces of evergreens – holly, ivy or cypress

Christmas tree ornaments

Florist's artificial holly berries – approximately 40

Pine cones

Floral wire, #18 gauge, enough for pine cones, ornaments, ribbon bows and bunches of berries

4½yd of 1½in-wide plaid ribbon for bows

Fine masonry nails

Evergreen garland

If the main focal point of your room is a fireplace, then you have the perfect setting for a truly traditional garland of evergreens and pine cones. The evergreen garland featured here does not, of course, have to be set over a fireplace: it could be arranged above a doorway or an arch, around picture frames or even around a window. If it could be swathed around a mirror then you would have the double benefit of the reflection.

Hanging

Start by deciding exactly where the garland is to hang and how. Fine masonry nails, of the type used to hang pictures, are very unobtrusive and should not leave any visible mark, but if you are worried about damaging your wall you may be able to avoid inserting new nails if you can use existing picture hooks.

Any nails should be hammered in at a slightly sloping angle for added strength.

When you have decided where the garland is to hang, loop a length of string in that position and then measure it to find how long your sash cord should be. Remember that the sprigs of evergreen at either end will increase the length to some extent. Cut the cord to the necessary length.

Making the garland

Take handfuls of the moss and wrap it around the cord, then bind it over and over with fine wire until you have made a moss-padded sausage shape about 10in in diameter. Measure the padded cording and mark the center point.

Cut even lengths of evergreens and group them into small mixed bunches – cypress, holly and ivy, for example – to make sure that you achieve an even distribution of the different types and colors along the length of the cord.

The next stage is to start binding the sprigs to the cord. If it is to lie flat

against the wall, then you will want to make sure that the sprigs lie at the front and sides. If the finished garland is to be draped over a mirror, bear in mind that the back will also be visible to some extent.

Start at the center of the rope and work first out to one end. Place a bunch of evergreens on the rope, with the stems toward the center, and bind it firmly in place, passing over and over the stems with the fine wire. Arrange each following bunch so that the stems are concealed by the tips of the previous one.

Reverse the rope and start from the center again, working out to the other end. Make a small cluster of leaves and bind them to the center of the garland to conceal the overlapping stems.

Finishing and mounting

Using floral wire, bind the holly berries together in small bunches,

leaving enough wire to attach each bunch to the garland. Wire the pine cones (see page 12) and thread floral wire through the loop at the back of each ornament.

Spacing them in an attractive but random pattern, push the wires holding the berries, cones and ornaments into the moss.

Cut a 1¼yd length of the ribbon and tie it into a bow for the center of the garland. Pass a wire through the loop at the back and push it into the moss. Cut the remaining ribbon into six equal lengths and form each into a bow, then wire them to the garland in the same way.

To hang the garland, wind lengths of wire around it at the hanging points, concealing the wire under the sprigs, and tie the wires firmly to the nails or picture hooks. Adjust the outer edges of the foliage to give a feathered look.

Evergreen candy wreath

Pretty and eye-catching, and with a tasty promise of things to come, this candy wreath would make a great gift, whatever the age of the recipient. A sweet tooth is the only prerequisite. Lacy posies of shiny wrapped pieces of candy adorn a ring of evergreen foliage interspersed with crosses bound with red satin ribbon.

The result is a charming wreath which can be hung on a wall or door or even placed in the center of the table as an exciting centerpiece, ready to be demolished at the end of the meal. If family and guests are content to feast only with their eyes, it can be saved as a last treat before the decorations come down.

If you have small children around, this wreath is too tempting to be kept for so long. Rather than risk accidents as young candy raiders stretch up from precariously balanced chairs, it would be safer to leave it within reach and face the lesser risk that it will be demolished!

The foliage

Choose thick, bushy sprigs of foliage. If necessary they can always be trimmed. The ring will look much more attractive if more than one type of foliage is used. The most suitable trees to choose would be some types of firs, using a dark variety for the background and overlaying this with sprigs taken from a tree or bush of a brighter green and with a slightly different growth pattern. If you wish to relieve the green, you could perhaps add a few sprigs from a golden cypress. If you do not have any fir trees and must buy your foliage, you'll need to trim the stems and

Materials
Ring
Ready-made florist's wire ring, 9in to 10in in diameter
or two rolls of green rubber-coated garden wire – one of medium thickness and one thinner and more pliable
Wire-cutting pliers
$4\frac{1}{2}$yd of black or dark green wide bias binding
Black or dark green tissue paper – enough to wrap around the ring in a loose spiral
Black or dark green thread
Selection of evergreen foliage sprigs, each 4in to 6in long
$3\frac{1}{4}$yd of $\frac{3}{8}$in-wide red satin ribbon

Posies
30 shiny wrapped pieces of candy – 15 each in red and green (if you want to use unwrapped chocolate truffles or after-dinner mints so that the wreath can form a table centerpiece for a dinner party, then use small quantities of foil paper in different colors)
$1\frac{1}{2}$yd of $1\frac{1}{2}$in-wide red satin ribbon to hang the ring
$1\frac{1}{2}$yd of ruffled eyelet trim
$1\frac{1}{2}$yd of green rubber-coated garden wire for tying

immerse the sprigs in water for a few hours before making the ring.

Making the ring

Using the thicker wire, make two rings, one 8in in diameter and one 10in, each formed from three circles of wire and held together with cellophane tape at four evenly spaced points.

Place the smaller ring inside the larger one and, using the thinner wire, lace them together by double-twisting the wire around each ring alternately, working progressively around until the two rings are firmly fixed together. Twist any sharp ends so that they point inward.

Take a sheet of tissue paper and loosely roll it up along its length, then very loosely twist the paper cylinder into a spiral. Lay it around the front of the wire circle to give bulk to the top (visible) side. You may find that you need to use more than one sheet of tissue paper to cover the entire circle.

Open out the bias binding and press it flat. Use the tape to bind the tissue paper to the rings, passing the tape in and out of the rings and working around in a spiral. Take care not to crush the paper, and overlap the previous round of binding by approximately a third of its width at each turn. In this way pockets will be formed into which the sprigs of foliage can be inserted.

Take the darker foliage first and strip off the lower leaves to expose about 1½in of stem. Working always in the same direction, insert the stems under the overlapping bands of binding. Build up the ring in this manner until it looks dense and bushy, finishing off with lighter-colored foliage. Use smaller sprigs to fill in any thin-looking areas.

When the ring looks well-covered, use the thread to bind around the foliage, placing the thread out of sight under the surface greenery. Any pieces that protrude beyond the others can be lightly pruned away.

The posies

Take dark thread and tie it first around the end of one piece of candy then bind it firmly to the next. Holding the ends firmly in the fingers of one hand, continue to tie on pieces of candy, winding the thread tightly around each one several times and in and out of the other pieces of candy in random directions until they are all firmly bound together at one end. Make six groups of candy in this manner.

Cut the ruffled eyelet trim into six 10in lengths and sew small running stitches along the ruffled edges. Gather each one up to measure 4in and fasten with several small stitches. Sew the raw edges together, forming a ruffled circle of lace.

Take each cluster of candy and twist a short length of wire around its base. Place the cluster inside the eyelet ring and fasten the whole posy very firmly to the fir wreath by winding the wire around the padded ring.

Finish off by cutting the narrow red ribbon into two equal lengths of 1⅝yd. Fasten the ends on the underside and, working in opposite directions, wind both lengths around

the ring so that they form a cross between each posy.

Use the wider ribbon to tie a bow at the top of the wreath.

Straw wreath

Based on the ancient country craft of making corn dolls – straw figures to symbolize the forces of fertility and ward away evil – here is a charmingly rural wreath festooned with loving hearts and Christmas stars to bring you luck now and in the coming year.

You can buy the various elements used in making this unusual hanging wreath from a craft store, but it would be infinitely more pleasant to gather them for yourself from the countryside on a warm afternoon in the late autumn and store them ready for the festive season. If you cannot find pine cones of the appropriate size you could wind trails of ivy around the ring, to alternate with the ribbon, or attach attractive dried seed heads taken from your yard.

Making the ring

First cut the birch twigs. The finished ring shown here measures approximately 14in in diameter and 31¼in thick, when bound. The twigs must be fresh and pliable (twigs found on the ground may be too brittle) and the leaves must be stripped off. If you do not have silver birches in your area, use other canes or twigs. (Sweet chestnut is very pliable, and it may help if you soak the twigs in water overnight.)

Form the twigs into a ring and bind them firmly together with garden twine. Make sure that the ring is completely symmetrical.

Take the grass or raffia and carefully bind it around the twigs until they are completely covered.

Wind the red ribbon around the ring in a spiral, leaving about 1in of

Materials

Silver birch twigs (or similarly pliable twigs)
Dried long, wild grass stalks (or use straw-colored raffia)
20 small pine cones
About 100 straw or wheat stalks – approximately 8in long
7¾yd of 1in-wide red ribbon
Thin cardboard
Red tissue paper
Gold star stickers (obtainable in sheets from stationery stores)
Garden twine
Straight pins
Cream and red sewing thread
All-purpose glue
Scissors
X-acto knife
Tracing paper

Trace pattern for hearts

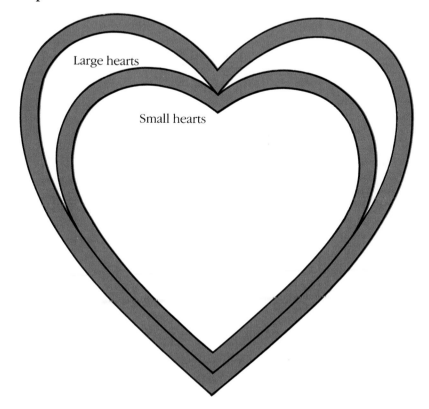

Large hearts

Small hearts

grass showing through between each turn of the ribbon. When you have worked around the ring, cut the ribbon and secure the ends with straight pins, stuck into the ring.

Attach the pine cones to the top of the ring with all-purpose glue, being careful to space them evenly around the circle.

The hearts

The hearts are all made in the same way. Trace over the heart outlines and either cut out the tracing paper shapes and use them as templates or use carbon paper to mark out five large hearts and three smaller ones on the cardboard. Cut these out.

Draw around the inside of each heart shape, ⅛in from the outer edge, and very carefully cut along this line to leave a narrow heart-shaped outline in cardboard.

Cover the outline lightly with glue and lay it down over red tissue paper.

If you have not used star stickers, you'll need to dab a tiny amount of glue on each one.

Cut out the heart shapes, then once more put glue around the cardboard edge and, turning the hearts over, place them on the tissue paper again so that both sides are now covered and the stars are enclosed. Cut around the outline of each heart once more.

Thread a needle with red sewing thread and make a neat knot at the end. Draw the needle through the center point at the top of a large heart so that it is held by the knot. Push the other end through the ring, so that the heart can hang down from the ring by a thread approximately 2¼in long. Suspend three more large hearts from the ring in the same way, spacing them an equal distance apart.

In the same way, link the remaining four hearts together: attach the center top of one small heart to the lower tip of the remaining large heart, leaving a ¾in length of thread between them; attach the center top of the large heart to the lower tip of another small heart, with a 1¼in length of thread between them; attach the remaining heart to the chain with the same spacing. Set this chain of hearts to one side.

Make sure that the paper is absolutely flat – if necessary press it first with a warm iron to remove any wrinkles. Position about six paper stars on each of the larger hearts, spacing them evenly but at random over the tissue paper, on the side with the cardboard.

Straw stars

Take the pieces of straw and flatten them with the blunt side of your X-acto knife, working from both sides of the straw until each piece is completely flat. To avoid damaging the work surface, cover it with newspaper or cardboard.

When you have several flattened straws, you can start making the stars. They are all made following the same principle but you can vary the stars by using different lengths and thicknesses of straw.

For the first type of star, take four pieces of straw approximately ¼in wide and 3½in long, and four thin straws approximately ⅛in wide and the same length as the others. Holding them steadily between thumb and forefinger, arrange two thin straws to cross each other at right angles, then add the other two to cross each other, lying in between the spaces left by the first two. Add the four thick straws to complete the star shape so that there are 16 spokes radiating outward, with thick and thin straws alternating.

Take about 20in of cream thread and, leaving an end approximately 6in in length, wrap the thread around one of the straws and tie a knot. Make the tie as close to the center of the star as possible and make sure that you do not crush the straw. Work around the center, carefully taking the thread alternately over and under successive straws, gently moving your finger and thumb out of the way as you work, but keeping a firm hold on the star. When you have worked all the way around and back to the beginning, wrap the thread around the first straw again and then repeat the process, this time working counter-clockwise and taking the thread under the straws that it passed over the first time, and vice versa.

Tie a knot and trim the thread so that both ends are 6in long. Trim the straws so that they are all the same length, then shape the points with a pair of sharp scissors. You can alternate points with inverted points, or clip them into arrow shapes, as shown.

Make several variations, working to the same basic method. Some of the stars shown here, for instance, are made by crossing 12 thin straws and cutting half of the spokes back to within ¾in of the center, so that long and short spokes alternate around the star.

Make a total of eight stars of varying forms. Thread the ends through a needle and attach the stars to the ring so that there are two evenly spaced stars between each heart.

Finishing

From the remaining ribbon cut two 30in lengths and attach them with straight pins inserted into the center of the ring, so that the four ends are evenly spaced and are secured at the points from which the four hearts will hang.

Take the remaining length of ribbon and tie it in a large bow at the point at which the two ribbons cross over. Leave one long end from which to hang the circle.

Using a needle and red thread, as before, run a length of thread through the center top of the first heart in the chain and take the other end through the central bow, so that the chain of hearts will be suspended from the center of the ring.

Shooting stars

Large gold or silver stars, linked with multicolored, star-scattered trails, make a dramatic room decoration, far more elegant and effective than the majority of purchased paper decorations. The stars are three-dimensional, made from carefully assembled pieces of gold cardboard. The number required and the length of trail to allow between stars will depend on the dimensions of your room, including the height of the ceiling, so before starting to make this decoration, experiment by holding paper streamers or even string against your walls to help you to get the proportions right. Once you have decided on the distance between the stars, these positions can be lightly marked using either a soft pencil or straight pins. Similarly, the choice of strands to make up the trails can be varied to suit your own particular color scheme and to match your other Christmas decorations. In fact, last year's paper streamers and tinsel may be given a new lease of life if used in this way.

Materials

16½in x 11½in piece of lightweight gold or silver cardboard for each star
Selection of rolls of crêpe paper and colored foil for the streamers
Lightweight gold or silver cardboard for small stars (optional)
Tracing paper and pencil
X-acto knife
Metal ruler
Clear glue

Small star

For best results, use templates to cut out these stars from gold and silver cardboard. Using a soft pencil and ruler, first trace the two stars shown and transfer the outlines to the cardboard, turning the tracing over before going over the outlines with a ruler and pencil. Cut out the templates using the X-acto knife and ruler. Make as many stars as necessary to decorate the trails.

Large star

The shape provided forms one point of a five-pointed star, so trace the shape and then transfer this to the back of the cardboard. Cut it out carefully, using the X-acto knife and metal ruler, then use this shape as a template to mark out as many points as you need for the number of stars.

On each point, the dashed lines represent folds; the dotted line marks the edge of tab 3, which is left flat and lies under the adjoining point. Carefully press along the foldlines with the blunt side of a knife or with a knitting needle, and then fold along these lines. Glue tab 1 under edge 1 to make a pointed shape with one raised side (the front) and one flat side (the back). Make four more points, then assemble them together by gluing tab 2 under the sloping edge 2 of the adjacent point and tab 3 under flat edge 3 until you have formed a five-pointed star.

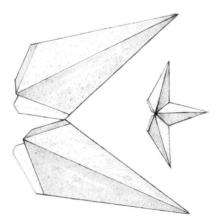

Trace pattern for small stars

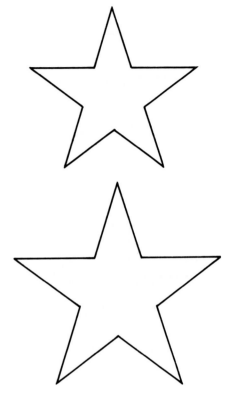

Trails

When you have as many stars as you need, make the looped trails, attaching them at the points which will be covered by the stars. Use a variety of strands of crêpe paper and colored foil, experimenting until you have a satisfactory effect. Place thicker strands at the back and lay thinner strands on top. Pin or tape the strands in position around the room then place the smaller, flat gold stars in between the trails, scattering them at random to give the effect of shooting stars.

Finishing

Finally, place the three-dimensional gold stars in position, with the flat center back of each star covering the point where the looped trails are attached to the wall. Use double-sided tape, reusable adhesive clay (such as Blu-Tack) or pieces of mount tape to hold the stars in position.

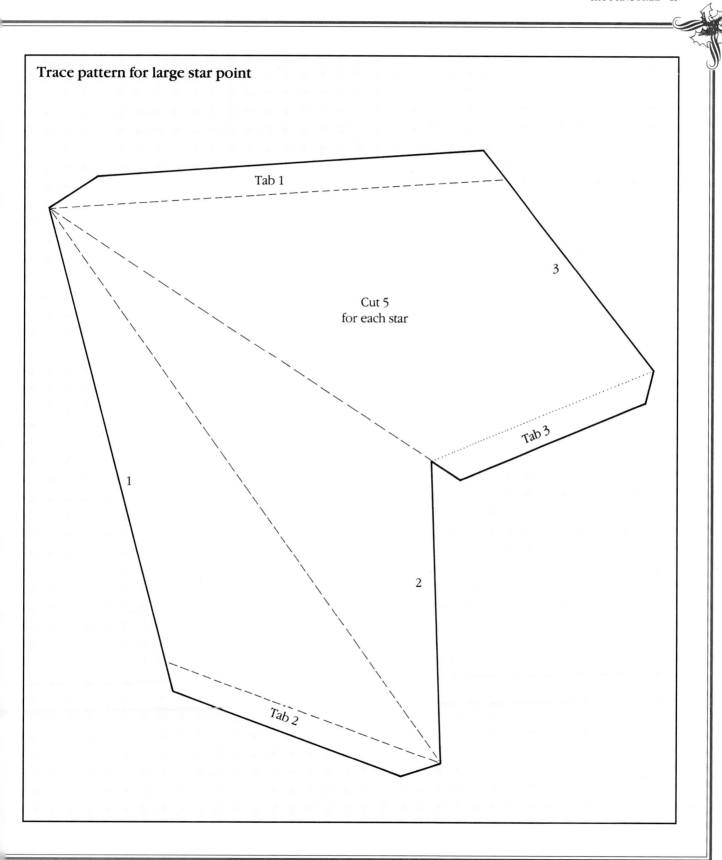

Trace pattern for large star point

Tab 1

3

Cut 5
for each star

Tab 3

1

2

Tab 2

CHAPTER 2

Christmas tree, oh Christmas tree

Decorating the Christmas tree is an important part of that gradual build-up of excitement that children find so exhilarating at Christmas – by the time you stand back to admire your efforts the suspense will have become almost unbearable! And how much more pleasurable the finished effect will be if you have made some or all of the decorations yourselves, as people used to do when Christmas trees first became popular. The decorations shown here include two alternative tree skirts, wooden outline figures, little wreaths and other tree hangings made from salt dough, patchwork stars, paper snowflakes and baskets, and padded angels and doves.

Materials

3/16in birch plywood scraps
Fine sandpaper
Satin finish varnish
Tracing paper
Pencils and pen
Fine artist's brush
Inks (see below)
Poster paints (see below)
Cellophane tape
Tissues
Gold thread
Santa Claus
Red ink
White, pink, blue and black poster
    paints
Angel
Yellow ink
White, pink, blue, black and gold
    poster paints
Star
Yellow ink
Snowman
White, black, green, red and
    orange poster paints
Heart
Red ink
Apple
Red, green and brown inks
Christmas tree
Green, red and brown inks
Candle
Green, red and yellow inks
White and black poster paints
Tools
Fret saw (or electric jigsaw)
Drill with small bit
Carpentry clamp

Wooden tree hangings

Easily made from plywood, these small shapes, brightly colored with poster paints, take very little time to make and no advanced carpentry skills. Use them as shown here, to decorate a tree, or for other Christmas decorations: you could hang snowmen, angels or Santas at the ends of a chain of cards, for instance, or you could make a mobile using lengths of silver or green rubber-coated garden wire for the cross-pieces.

Santa Claus
Copy the pattern onto tracing paper with a pencil. On the back side of the tracing paper, draw over the lines with a soft pencil. Place the tracing on the wood, with the soft pencil lines facing down, and using a harder pencil trace over the lines, transferring the design to the wood.

Drill a small hole at the top of the hat, just below the pompon, to take the thread.

Secure the wood to a solid surface, using the clamp (if you are using a good table, put cardboard between the gripping ends of the clamp and the table, to protect the surface). Carefully cut around the outline with the fret saw, taking care not to split the wood at the edges of the shape. Sandpaper around the edges, the front and the back.

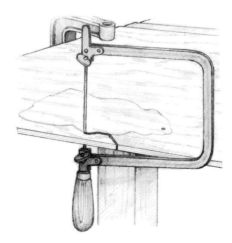

Using the fine brush and red ink, paint in all the red areas on the front of the design. Take great care where the red ends and another color begins to make sure that the red does not bleed along the grain of the wood.

You can help to reduce this problem by dabbing away excess ink with a tissue each time you have made a brush stroke. Ink around the edges of the shape, to fit in with the line of the costume, then leave the shape until the ink has dried thoroughly. Turn the shape over and, still using the red ink, paint the red areas on the back of the figure.

Mix white paint to a fairly thick but still paintable consistency and apply it carefully to the front and edges, where appropriate. As with the red ink, leave the paint to dry before turning the shape over and painting the white areas on the back.

Repeat the process with the black paint for the belt and boots, the pink paint for the cheeks, and the blue for the eyes.

When the paint is completely dry, paint the front and edges with the varnish and leave it to dry. Turn the shape over and repeat the process on the back. Give the decoration two complete coats of varnish.

Cut an 8in length of gold thread, push one end through the hole and make a tie.

Angel
Trace and cut out the shape as for Santa Claus. Paint the yellow ink on the front and edges of the wings and, when dry, on the back. As when applying the red ink to Santa Claus, use a tissue to dab any excess ink away as you paint.

Next apply poster paints in the following order: white for the dress, black for the hair, pink for the cheeks, blue for the eyes and gold for the halo and the dress details. Always paint the front and sides first and leave this layer to dry before turning the shape over and painting the back.

Varnish and hang the angel as described for Santa Claus.

Star
Make the star in the same way as for Santa Claus, using yellow ink for the front, edges and back.

Snowman
Trace and cut out the snowman as described for Santa Claus. Apply the paints in the following order: white, red, green, black and then orange. In each case, paint the front and edges first, then turn the piece over when the paint has dried and paint the back, before moving to the next color.

Finish with two coats of varnish and thread with a gold tie, as for the other shapes.

Heart
Make in the same way as the other shapes, using red ink for coloring.

Apple
Make in the same way as the other shapes. Apply the paints in the following order: red, green and then brown. In each case, paint the front and edges first, then turn the piece over when the paint has dried and paint the back.

Trace patterns for wooden tree hangings

Angel 1

Angel 2

Star

Heart

Santa
Claus

Apple

Snowman

Materials

A selection of bronze, gold and silver papers is generally used, or you might decide to make all your baskets from either a mixed variety of colors or just two colors, to match your chosen Christmas décor – gold and blue, for instance, or silver and red. For one basket you will need:

8½in x 4¼in piece of paper in each of two colors
Tracing paper
Ruler, pencil and felt-tipped pen
Paper scissors or X-acto knife
Paper glue
Medium-weight cardboard

Heart baskets

These pretty little paper baskets are so easy to make that they are quite simply child's play – a traditional pre-Christmas pastime for generations of children over the last century. The technique is so simple and effective that it takes very little time to produce several baskets, made from a variety of colored papers. Although they are made only from paper, each basket is sturdy enough to hold a few pieces of candy or chocolates or small gifts for a children's party.

Paper weaving

If you plan to make a whole collection of baskets for your tree, you will need to make a template from thin cardboard. Start by tracing the basket pattern given below. Glue the tracing to the cardboard and carefully cut out using a ruler and, if you have one, an X-acto knife to cut all straight edges, and taking care when cutting in between the inner strips. (See making a template on page 43.)

Place the template on colored paper with the short edge on a fold, as directed, and cut out. To avoid wasting paper, place each shape next to each other, butting up the straight edges.

The next stage may sound complicated, but in fact it is very easy to do if you have the pieces of paper ready to use. Take the two main pieces and hold them at right angles to each other, with the folded ends adjacent. Take the first folded strip of color 1 and push it through the first folded strip of color 2. Open the first strip of color 1 a little to make a loop, and pass the second strip of color 2 through the loop. Close the loop of color 1 and push it through the loop of the third strip of color 2, then push the last strip of color 2 through the loop of color 1.

One strip of the first color has now been woven into the second piece of paper. Repeat the process with the three remaining strips, alternating the process to create a woven effect. When the last strip is woven in, the

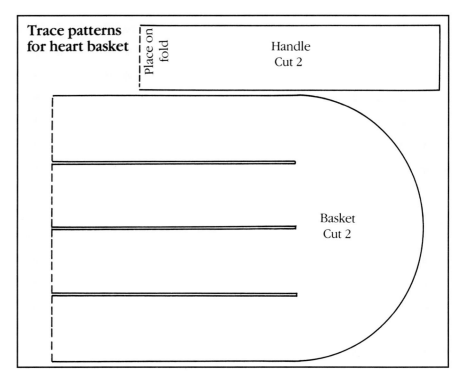

Trace patterns for heart basket

Place on fold

Handle
Cut 2

Basket
Cut 2

basket will hold itself in a secure shape when opened.

Glue the two strips for the handle together with wrong sides facing to make a two-colored handle strip, then glue the handle to the basket, with one end at the center of each side of the heart, and placing the ends about ¾in inside the basket.

Hang the basket on your tree with pieces of candy or a small gift inside.

You can vary the weaving pattern by taking some strips over two strips instead of one of the second color.

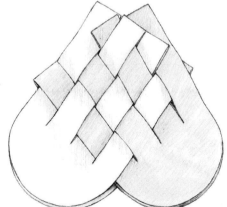

Snowflakes

Light, delicate snowflakes hanging from a tree or festooned around a room make delightfully pretty decorations. The outlines seen here are copied from real snowflake crystals, which appear in an infinite variety. The snowflakes themselves are designed in such a way that they can be as simple or as complicated as you wish: single crystal shapes to hang against a wall, or three-dimensional flakes formed from two, or for maximum effect three, interlocking circles. The flakes seen here are made from plain white cardboard and poster board, but you could equally well use tinfoil (two sheets glued together would make double-sided foil with extra strength) or colored cardboard or poster board.

Preparation

There are six spokes on a snowflake crystal, and the three-dimensional snowflakes are made up from quarter crystals, each with one and a half spokes, glued to central circles of cardboard. The single snowflake can either be formed from four quarters glued to a central cardboard circle, or you can cut it out in one piece, in which case you will not need a cardboard circle.

To transfer the outline to the poster board you can use one of several methods: if the poster board is transparent enough it may be possible simply to place it over the outline and trace through; or if this isn't possible, you could trace the outline and make a cardboard template (see page 43), or you could trace the outline and then transfer it to poster board The tracing can be used repeatedly if you turn it over after each use and trace down from the other side. Any pencil smudges on the poster board can easily be removed after you have cut out the shape.

The single snowflakes are four separate or repeated quarters; the

double flake is made from eight separate quarters, joined with two cardboard circles (these only require slit A in order to interlock), and the elaborate snowflake is made up from 12 pattern quarters plus three cardboard circles, one of each type shown. Although the pattern quarters needed to make up the double and elaborate snowflakes can all be of the same type, you may prefer to vary the effect, for example by using four of one type and four of another to make up the double snowflake.

If you take care when cutting out the outlines it is possible to cut out two layers at once from poster board, so you only have to mark out half the total number of outlines which you will need.

Cut out the snowflake pattern quarters and interlocking circles, using an X-acto knife. First cut out the shapes roughly, cutting about ⅜in outside the marked outer line. Cut the second, unmarked layer of cardboard approximately ¼in larger all around than the marked layer and tape both to a spare piece of fiberboard or similar small cutting surface which you can turn as you work.

Simple snowflake

Cut out a whole snowflake pattern or cut four quarters and glue these to a central circle. Gently erase any

Materials

Poster board for the crystal-shaped outlines – the amount will depend on the number and form of flakes desired

Medium cardboard for the central, interlocking circles

Tracing paper and pencil

X-acto knife

Clear glue

Transparent thread, for hanging

Sewing needle

Trace patterns for snowflake quarters

Trace patterns for central circles

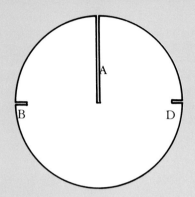

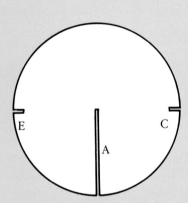

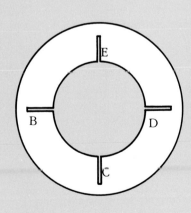

remaining pencil lines, then using the needle and thread make a hanger through the end of one of the crystal spokes.

Double snowflake

Take two cardboard circles, each with slot A cut out, and fit them together through the slot into a spherical shape. Glue four snowflake quarters to each circle. Hang the snowflake as already described.

Elaborate snowflake

Cut three cardboard circles, one with slots A, B and D, one with A, C and E, and one hollow circle with B, C, D and E. Interlock the first two through slot A, then carefully slip the third circle over the resulting spherical shape until it locks into position through the side slots.

Take twelve pattern quarters of the type given for the elaborate snowflake and position four around each cardboard circle. Hang the snowflake as already described.

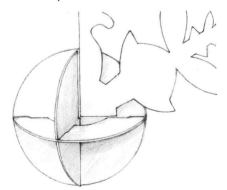

Materials

Medium-thick cardboard – approximately
   4in x 8in
Tracing paper
Spray glue
X-acto knife
Metal ruler
Writing paper
Small quantities of at least six
   dress-weight cotton fabrics
Small quantity of loose batting
Matching sewing thread

Templates for stars

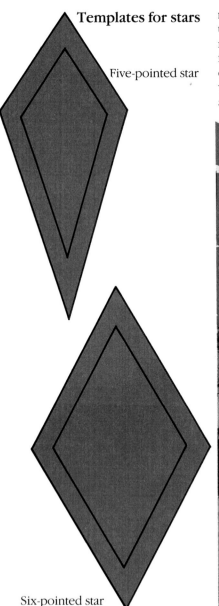

Five-pointed star

Six-pointed star

Stars, stars, stars

Give your Christmas tree a traditional
look by festooning it with these dainty
patchwork stars instead of the more
usual commercially produced
ornaments. Here are decorations
which are easy to make at odd
moments, and in fact because they are
sewn by hand you can even carry the
work around with you.

The five- and six-pointed stars are
made by joining diamonds together
using the English backing paper
method, which gives a very precise
finish – ideal for these neat little
decorations which will twinkle on
your tree year after year. You can use
small odds and ends from your scrap
bag, but it would be better to choose
small amounts (the minimum
quantities that you can buy) of co-
ordinating Christmas fabrics. Make
sure that all the fabrics are the same
quality and weight; ideally, dress-
weight pure cotton.

Make as many stars as you need for
your tree, plus a few extra ones to tuck
into your Christmas wreath and other
decorations, to carry the theme
through.

Five-pointed star

The five-pointed star is made with the
two more sharply pointed templates,
with the sharp points facing outwards.
Start by making two cardboard
templates. The smaller template will

be used to cut the backing papers; the larger template is used for the fabric shapes and therefore includes the seam allowances.

Trace over the two diamond shapes given then cut them out roughly, leaving a margin of about ⅜in around each shape. Using spray glue, stick the tracing paper shapes to the cardboard, then carefully cut out the templates along the marked lines, leaning the X-acto knife against the metal ruler.

Making the stars
Each star is made from a total of ten diamonds – five for the front and five for the back.

Using the smaller template, mark as many diamonds as you will need for the desired number of stars on the writing paper and cut them out. Using the larger template, mark and cut out an equal number of fabric patches, making sure that you distribute the patches evenly between the different fabrics.

To prepare the patches, place a backing paper in the center of a fabric patch on the wrong side, and hold them together with a pin. Fold the seam allowances over the backing paper one by one and baste. Fold the seams in neatly at the wide angles, but allow the excess seam allowances to lie flat at the sharp points, so that they protrude beyond the backing papers.

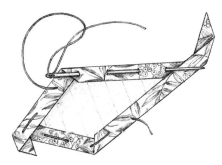

Place two diamonds right sides together and whipstitch along one edge, making 20 stitches to the inch. Do not stitch beyond the point of the backing paper. Sew another

pair together, then whipstitch the two pairs together. Add one more diamond to complete the star shape.

Make sure that the protruding tails all follow in the same direction so that they interlock neatly at the center of the star, each tail lying over the tail of the preceding diamond.

When you have made two star shapes, pin them right sides together and whipstitch along the edges, folding and trimming as necessary to make neat points. Leave a small gap unsewn and turn the star right side out through this gap, after first taking out the basting and removing the backing papers by pulling them gently loose from the stitches.

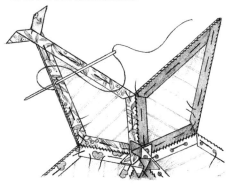

Gently ease out the points, using a knitting needle or a blunt pencil and push a little batting into the star. Make sure that it is evenly distributed, right up to the points, and do not overfill. Sew the opening closed.

To attach a loop for hanging, simply thread a needle with matching thread or fine metallic thread and insert it through one of the points, about ¼in from the tip. Cut the thread to the right length and then knot the ends together.

Six-pointed star
The six-pointed stars are made in exactly the same way as the others, but using the two remaining diamond templates. Make each star shape by sewing three pairs of patches together, and then sewing the pairs together to form a six-pointed star.

Materials

For each bird
Tracing paper
Medium-weight cardboard
Spray glue
1/4yd of 36in-wide polyester satin
Loose polyester batting
1 yd of 1/8in-diameter pearl trim
Two flower sequins
Two rhinestones
Fabric glue
Matching sewing thread

White bird
1/2yd of 1/8in-wide white-and-silver
   ribbon
3/4yd of 3/8in-wide ruffled lace trim

Blue bird
3 1/4yd of 1/8in-wide white ribbon
1 yd of 1/8in-wide white ribbon

Peach bird
Six lace motifs
3/4yd of gold (picot) trim
1/2yd of gold cording
1/2yd of 1/8in-wide gold ribbon
2 gold beads

Flight of fantasy

Doves of peace in white, peach or blue satin make highly appropriate but unusual Christmas decorations. Make a complete set to hang from a large tree, or just a single bird to decorate a Christmas wreath. The different trims added here are only suggestions – this is a chance to delve into your scrap basket for odds and ends of trimmings that were too pretty to discard. The finished doves measure approximately 5in deep and 8in from tip to tail, but if this is too large for your purposes make your templates smaller, adjusting the cutting and stitching lines, as desired.

White bird

Trace the diagrams for the wing and body onto tracing paper, glue the paper to medium-weight cardboard with spray glue and cut around the outlines to make templates.

Using the templates to transfer the outlines onto the fabric, cut out one pair of bodies and two pairs of wings. Make sure that the grainlines of the fabric will all run in the same direction on the finished birds.

Place the two body pieces with right sides together and stitch around the outline, making a 1/4in seam and leaving an opening for turning, as

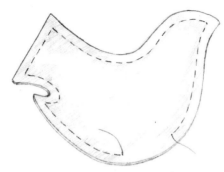

indicated. Sew the two pairs of wings together in the same manner, again leaving openings for turning. Cut notches from the seam allowances on outward curves and clip almost to the stitching line on inward curves then

turn the pieces right side out. Fill the pieces with batting and slip stitch the openings together.

The eyes and trims, as well as the wings, are all attached with fabric glue. This must be done very carefully, so that no glue ends up in the wrong place. If any should get on your hands or the work surface, clean it away before continuing. Use a toothpick or a blunt-ended tapestry needle to apply the glue in fine lines.

Glue lace to the back of each wing, overlapping the lace neatly at the wing tips. Apply pearl trim to the outer edge of each wing, so that it is backed by the lace. Again, start and finish at the wing tips.

Glue pearl trim around the body, covering the seamline. Apply a flower sequin at each eye position, then add a rhinestone to the center.

Glue the wings in position on the body. Cut a 10in length of narrow white-and-silver ribbon, form it into a loop to make a hanger and glue the ends in position, as indicated on the diagram.

Take the remaining length of ribbon around the neck and form it into an unknotted bow. Glue it in position to complete the bird.

Blue and peach birds

The blue and peach birds are made in the same way as the white bird but with different trims. For the blue bird, glue strips of white ribbon to the wings before applying the pearl trim and tie a single bow around the neck. For the tails to the bow, cut two 16in lengths each of blue and white ribbon, fold in half and glue in place. (You may prefer to hold these lengths of ribbon together with a few small stiches rather than glue.)

For the peach bird, attach gold picot braid to the wings in place of the lace trim of the white bird, and gold cording in place of the pearl trim. Glue lace motifs in position as shown in the photograph. Use gold ribbon for a neck tie and a hanging loop.

Trace pattern for bird

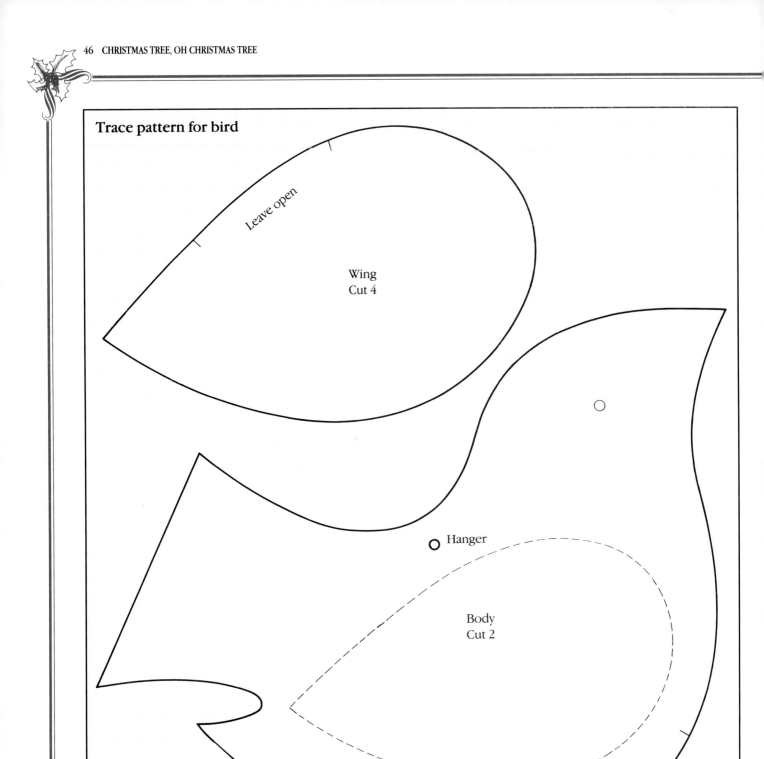

Leave open

Wing
Cut 4

○ Hanger

Body
Cut 2

Leave open

Band of angels

Make a little band of angels with round, smiling faces to hang from your tree and add a touch of home-produced cheerfulness. Each angel carries a different instrument or accessory, ingeniously made from such unlikely beginnings as a golf tee, and each is decorated with delicate hand embroidery and gold trimmings. The angels are not difficult to make, though the embroidery takes a little time, and you and your family can all have fun thinking up further home-made musical instruments for the band.

The angels are all made in the same basic way, but their expressions, instruments and dress embroidery serve to individualize them.

Making the head

Using the permanent marker, draw a face on the large macramé bead (the drilled hole must run from top to bottom of the finished head). If you do not feel very confident about the result, draw the face in very lightly with pencil first so that you can erase or wipe off any mistakes.

Pick out the wire strands of the pot scrubber and cut away about a third. Glue the scrubber to the bead so that it frames the face.

The embroidery

Mark an oblong on the unbleached muslin measuring 7¼in x 4in, using the ruler and pencil. Decide which embroidery pattern you wish to use – each dot on the pattern represents one French knot – and again using the pencil, lightly indicate the pattern on the unbleached muslin. Place the lowest points ⅜in up from one long marked edge (this becomes the bottom edge) and make all markings on the wrong side of the fabric.

Using coton perlé thread, embroider the pattern of your choice, making French knots and long straight stitches where indicated.

French knots

To work French knots, bring the thread out at the desired position and hold it down to one side with the left thumb. Twist the thread twice around the needle, then insert the needle into the fabric close to the starting point. Pull it through to the back, tightening the knot, and bring it out ready for the next knot.

The body

Cut out the fabric oblong and also a circle measuring 2⅛in in diameter. Place the muslin strip with right sides together and short ends matching and machine stitch, making a ¼in seam. Press the seam open.

Pin the circle into the lower end of the tube and stitch in place, again making a ¼in seam. Turn the tube right side out.

Turn down a ¼in seam allowance at the top end of the tube and run a gathering thread around. Fill the tube with polyester batting and pull the gathers up tightly. Fasten off.

To make the arms, trim the pipe cleaner to 6¾in and glue a small wooden bead to each end. Mark and cut out a strip of unbleached muslin 7in x 2⅛in. Turn under a ¼in seam allowance along each short edge and press in place. Fold the strip in half lengthwise and machine stitch down the long edge with a ¼in seam. Turn the tube right side out and work a row of French knots around each pressed edge. Slip the pipe cleaner into the tube.

The wings

Cut a 7in square of unbleached muslin, and also cut a piece of fusible web 7in x 3½in. Place the fusible web on the wrong side of the muslin and fold the muslin over it, sandwiching the web between layers of muslin. Press well, until the web has firmly fused the muslin together.

Trace over the outline of the wings, glue the paper to cardboard and cut out to make a template. Mark around

Materials

For each angel
1½in-diameter wooden macramé bead
Two 1½in-diameter wooden beads
18in x 8in piece of unbleached muslin
DMC coton perlé No. 5 in cream #712
Brass wire pot scrubber
One pipe cleaner
¾in of gold cording
Fusible web
Loose polyester batting
Permanent marker (black)
All-purpose glue (use a glue gun
    if you have one)
Pinking shears (optional)
Medium-weight cardboard
Tracing paper
Ruler and pencil
Cream-colored sewing thread
Trumpet player
Gold spray
Golf tee
Drummer
Styrofoam circle 1in in diameter
    and ⅝in deep
⅛in-wide gold tape
⅜yd of fine gold cording
Two wooden cocktail sticks
Two small wooden beads
Singer
1in x 2in piece of gold cardboard

French knots

the template with a pencil onto the muslin.

Glue the gold cording to the muslin, covering the marked pencil outline. Cut out the wing shape, cutting as close to the cording as possible using pinking shears.

Finishing

Take an 8½in length of gold cording and fold it in half to form a loop. Attach the ends to the top of the body either with glue or with a few stitches. Thread the hanger through the head, bringing it out carefully through the wire hair.

Glue the head to the top of the body. With centers matching, glue the arm section to the body, at the back of the neck. Bring the arms to the front.

Glue the wings to the back of the body covering the arm join. The wings can be glued with the wing tips either pointing upward, as with the trumpet player, or downward, as with the other two angels.

Complete each angel by adding the appropriate accessory, gluing it in place. For the trumpet player, spray the golf tee with gold, then glue it to the bead hands. For the singer, fold the gold cardboard in half, first scoring the foldline on the right side, open it out slightly and glue it to the hands.

For the drummer, first glue fine gold tape around the top and bottom of the drum. Take a short length of the cording and glue it in a zigzag pattern with the V shapes running around the sides of the drum between the two bands of gold. Glue the remaining length of fine gold cording to the drum to make a hanger, first passing it around the neck of the angel. Trim the cocktail sticks to about ½in and glue a small wooden bead to one end of each stick. Push the drumsticks into the bead hands and add a little glue to hold them in place.

Variations

There are many other instruments which could be devised if you want to extend the band to more than these three angels. You could, for example, form a small circle out of brass picture hanging wire around a cardboard base and glue sequins around the edge at intervals, to make a tambourine. You could also use the same wire to make a percussion triangle, using a brass pin for a beater.

If you wish the angels to be free-standing instead of hanging from a tree, omit the hanger and cut out a cardboard circle, ½in smaller in diameter than the muslin circle for the base, and insert the cardboard into the base before adding the batting.

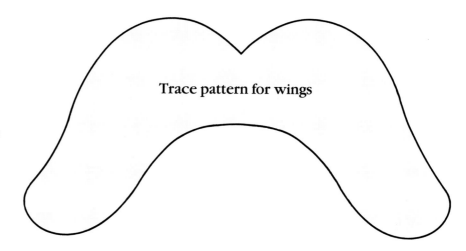

Trace pattern for wings

Trace pattern for embroidery

Drummer

Trumpet player

Singer

Dough
1lb all-purpose flour
½lb salt
1½cups water

Materials
Tracing paper
Medium-weight cardboard
Spray glue
X-acto knife
Red and green food coloring
Silver and gold paints (optional)
Pastry brush
Red and green parcel ribbon for hanging
Clear varnish (optional)

Floral tree decorations

Salt dough – a hard, inedible dough made from flour and salt – is used for these pretty, old-fashioned floral tree hangings. The pieces are very easy to make – definitely a potential family activity – and the modeling and varnishing make a pleasant occupation for a winter's afternoon or evening. Do not make the decorations too thick, or they may hang heavily on your tree, and adjust the size of the pieces to the scale of the tree. If you have a little girl's stocking to fill, save a small quantity of the dough and model some Christmas fare for her doll's house – a turkey, a fruitcake or a plum pudding.

Making templates
First trace the main outlines of the shapes, tracing around the outer edge of the basket and the bouquet and around the outside and the inner circle of the wreath. Also, make templates for the leaves and flowers.

If you want to make the decorations larger or smaller, draw the outlines to a larger or smaller scale as follows: to make the outlines 50 per cent smaller, first draw a grid on the tracing paper, each square measuring ¾in both ways. Take a second sheet of tracing paper and draw a grid, this time of ⅜in squares. Working square by square, transfer the outlines of the decorations to the second, smaller grid, thus reducing them by half.

When you have drawn your outlines to the desired size, cut out the shapes, leaving a margin of about ⅜in all around each one. Using spray glue, attach the traced outlines to cardboard and carefully cut out the shapes, this time cutting along the lines.

Modeling the dough
First make the salt dough: mix all the ingredients together to form a fairly stiff dough. Leave the dough in a plastic bag in the refrigerator overnight.

The following day, knead the dough very thoroughly by hand, then divide it in half. Take one half of the dough and roll it out on a floured board to an even thickness of about ³⁄₁₆in.

Using the cardboard templates and an X-acto knife, carefully cut around the outlines and remove the center from the wreath. Braids are made from three rolls twisted together. Make as many shapes as you can, then remove the spare dough and use this and the portion previously set aside to model the flowers, berries, leaves and baskets.

Divide the dough, allowing a large amount for green and smaller for red, and place it in separate mixing bowls. Add enough food coloring to make the green and red of your choice, and mix thoroughly.

The basic shapes make bases for the modeled pieces, and add to the three-dimensional quality of the decorations. Take small pieces of the appropriate color and use the templates to cut leaf and flower shapes. Add texture and other details by hand, using a knife or the tip of a pencil where necessary. To stick the modeled pieces to the bases, dampen the base and the underside of the piece to be attached to it, and score both lightly with a fork.

While you are forming the various components of the decorations it may be necessary to sprinkle the dough with flour to prevent it from becoming too sticky. Use only as much flour as is absolutely necessary and do not leave any loose flour on the surface: brush any excess away with a pastry brush. The diagrams are only a general guide: it would be attractive to vary the arrangements a little within the outlines so that no two decorations are identical.

Use the blunt end of a toothpick or a small screwdriver to make the holes in the top of the finished bouquets and wreaths to take the ribbons for hanging. Use an X-acto knife to cut away the space beneath the handle of each basket.

When you have finished modeling all the pieces, leave them on a wooden board or a baking tray for a minimum of 24 hours to allow them to dry out, then bake them in an oven at 325° for one hour. After this, leave them on a baking tray to cool before varnishing.

Finishing

When the pieces are cool, varnish the surfaces with a brush. Allow them to dry thoroughly before varnishing the undersides.

Cut a 14in length of ribbon for each decoration and thread it through the hole at the top to make a hanger.

**Trace patterns for
floral tree decoration**

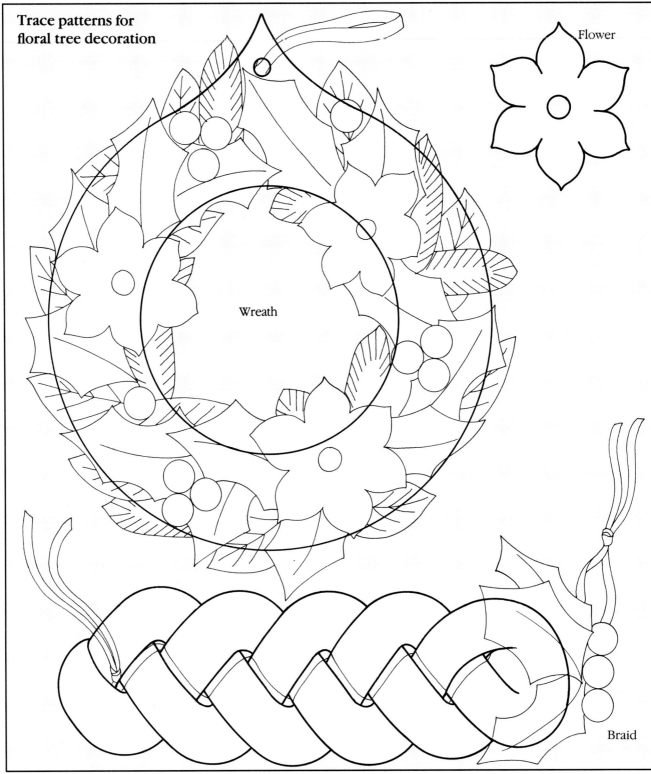

Flower

Wreath

Braid

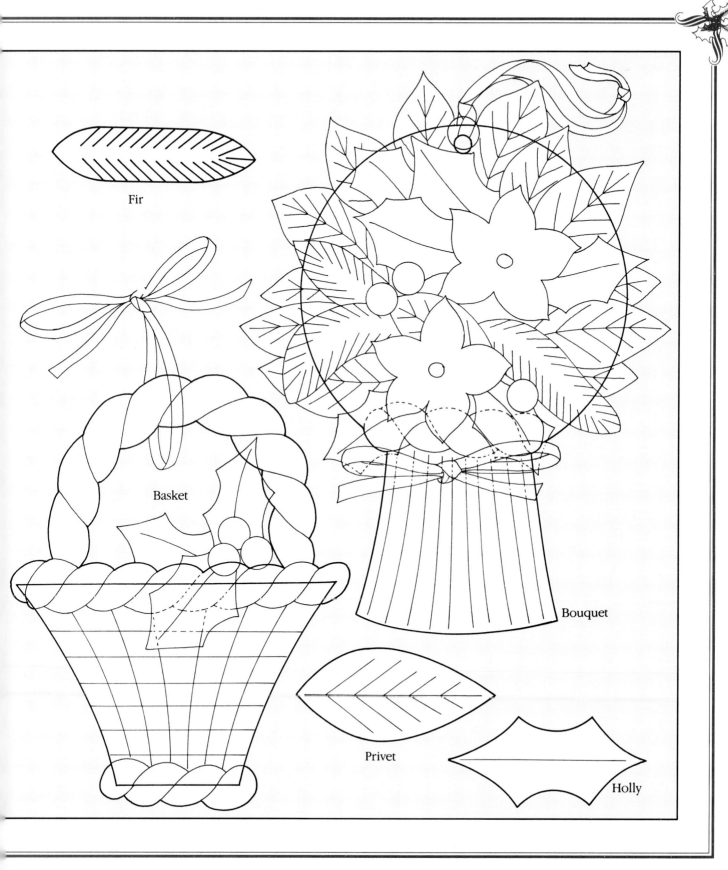

Fir

Basket

Bouquet

Privet

Holly

Materials

1⅝yd of 60in-wide green felt
⅜yd of 45in-wide gold Lurex fabric
6¾yd of 2in-diameter 8-ply gold tinsel
11yd of ¾in-wide flexible gold braid
1⅝yd of ⅛in-wide green ribbon
8 gold bells
Medium-weight cardboard
Large sheet of paper, at least
    27½in square
Protractor, long ruler and set square
Tracing paper
Pencil
Tailor's chalk marking pencil
Gold and green sewing thread
Stapler and staples (optional)

Cutting felt circle

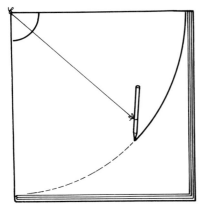

Gilded tree skirt

Plain green felt and gold trim are used to make this stunning tree skirt, with small gold bells added to the large stars to provide a touch of frivolity. The skirt shown here measures approximately 55in in diameter, though it could easily be scaled down for a smaller tree. Change the colors, if necessary, to suit your décor: a pale icy blue with silver trimmings would look very striking for example, or for a richer effect you could contrast midnight blue with gold.

Stars

Start by preparing the stars. Trace the outlines and glue the tracings to cardboard with spray glue then cut out two templates, one for the large star and one for the smaller star.

Using the templates, draw four large stars and four smaller ones on the wrong side of the Lurex fabric. Leave enough space around each outline to allow for a ¼in seam allowance to be added. Set your machine to straight stitch and sew along the marked outlines. Cut out the stars, adding a seam allowance around each one.

Using a fine needle and thread in order not to damage the fabric, turn under the seam allowance around each star and baste it in place. Turn the raw edges under following the machine stitched line, making sure that this will not show from the right side.

Clip up to the stitching line at the V shapes, and miter the points of the stars as you baste: first turn down the point of the star, folding at the stitched point, then turn under first one side and then the other. Fold the sides in carefully so that the seam allowance does not show.

Set the prepared stars to one side. It is a good idea to keep them in a separate plastic bag so that they receive as little handling as possible before they are attached to the skirt – many Lurex fabrics tend to ravel easily.

If your fabric is very prone to this, it might be safer to attach the stars with machine zigzag stitch, using a gold-colored thread or a thread chosen to match the felt. In this case, you could iron dress-weight fusible interfacing to the backs of the star shapes before you cut them out, which would hold the threads and prevent them from raveling.

Cutting the felt

The felt is first cut into a circle and then the outer edge is shaped into six large inverted scallops.

Start by trimming the felt to measure 55in square, then take the tailor's chalk marking pencil and attach a length of string to this. Knot the other end of the string: the length between the marking pencil and the knot should measure 27½in. Fold the fabric in half and then in half again to find the center. With the fabric still folded, hold the knot at the center point of the fabric and draw an arc on the folded fabric. Now tie the string again, to leave a length of 4in between the pencil and the knot, and draw a second arc on the still folded fabric.

Cut through all four layers of fabric along both arcs and open the felt out. You should now have a 55in diameter circle of felt, with a smaller circle cut away from the center.

If you find it difficult to cut through so many layers at once, find the center by first folding the fabric, then open it out and mark both complete circles on the fabric.

To make a pattern for the scallops, take the sheet of paper and trim it if necessary to make it 27½in square. Check the corners with a set square to make sure that they are right angles. From one corner draw a line on the paper at an angle of 60°. Take string and an ordinary pencil, the string knotted to leave a 27½in length. Holding the knot at the corner with the marked angle, draw an arc from the marked line to the edge of the paper, to make a shape which will be a

sixth of the felt circle. Cut out this pattern piece.

Lay the felt flat and place the pattern on it so that only the curve of the arc lies over the fabric and the ends of the curve lie exactly on the edge of the felt circle. Using the marking pencil, mark around the pattern, making one scallop shape on the fabric. Move the pattern around and mark a second scallop, starting from one end of the first. Move around the circle until you have marked six scallops.

Cut out the scallop shapes, then cut through the center of one scallop to the inner circle.

Attaching the trims

First baste and then machine stitch the braid around the edge of the skirt, using straight stitch and sewing along each side of the braid, as close to the edge as possible. The braid should be positioned 2¾in in from the outer edge, following the line of the scallops.

Make a neat fold at the beginning and end of each scallop, in order to carry the braid smoothly around. Start and finish at the edges of the slit, folding the raw ends of the braid under, to finish them.

Next pin the stars randomly but

Continue the same color scheme through your tree decorations simply by decorating the branches with green and gold ornaments and gold stars. Using the smaller template, cut the stars from gold cardboard, and make hanging loops using a needle and fine gold thread.

Trace patterns for stars

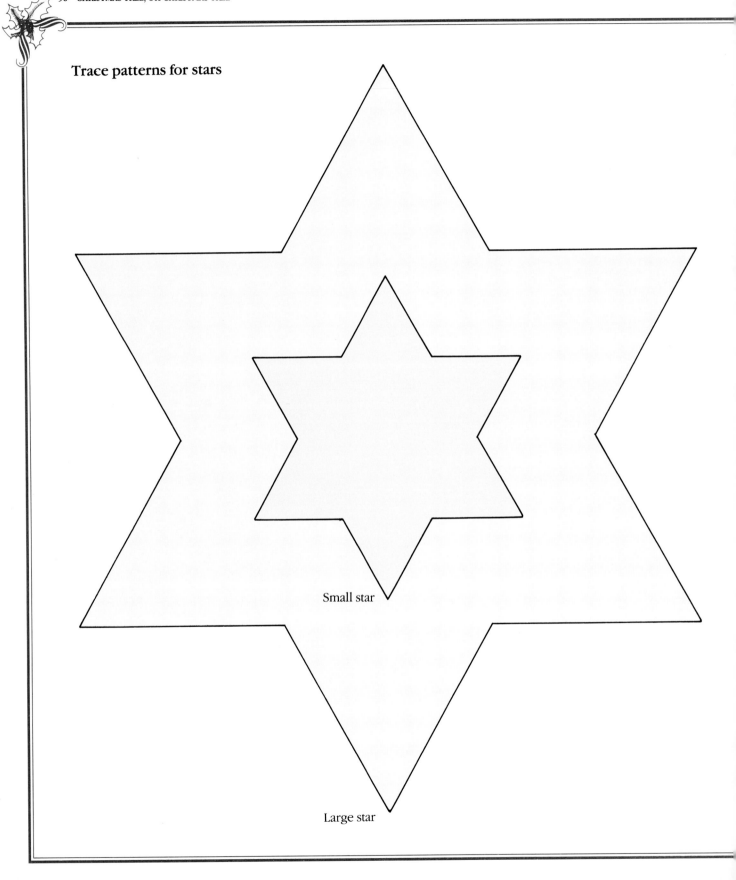

Small star

Large star

evenly spaced on the skirt, then baste them in place: begin by making large basting stitches out toward the points, starting in the center. Do not make knots at the center, but leave a long tail of thread, work out to one point, then rethread the needle at the center and baste out to the opposite point. When you have basted from the center, baste around the edge of each star, about 3/16in from the fold.

Using matching gold sewing thread, appliqué the stars to the felt using a very tiny blindstitch, taking the needle first into the felt and then exactly into the folded edge of the star. Check frequently to make sure that no stitches show, and make several small stitches at points which have been clipped to the seamline. When all the stars are attached, remove basting.

Cut the green ribbon into four equal lengths. Take a length of ribbon and thread it down and up through the center of one large star, leaving two equal lengths of ribbon at the front. Thread a gold bell onto each ribbon and then tie the ends into a knot to hold the bells firm. Form the ends of the ribbon into a bow, and catch the bow into position with a few small stitches. Repeat, to attach bells and bows to the center of each of the other large stars.

Starting at the slit, staple tinsel around the inner curve of the tree skirt, then around the outer, scalloped edge. A staple applied about every 3in will be enough to hold the tinsel in place. If you do not have a stapler, attach the tinsel with green thread, running long stitches around the under side of the skirt and bringing the needle up at intervals to secure the tinsel with tiny holding stitches not seen from the right side.

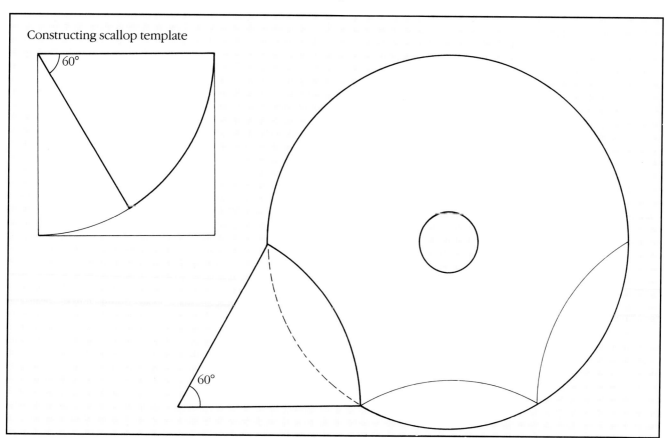

Constructing scallop template

Materials

1⅝yd of 60in-wide white felt
3¼yd of 36in-wide medium-weight
    fusible interfacing (optional – to be
    used if colored felt is thin and lacks
    body)
6½yd each of 1in-wide red and green,
    flexible wool braid
11yd of ⅛in-wide black soutache or
    similar narrow braid trim
Two 8in squares of yellow felt
One 8in square of felt each in red,
    cream, maroon, dark brown, beige,
    dark blue, gray, dark green, emerald
    and purple
Scraps of felt in mid brown, dark
    tan, gold, dark gold, yellow, light
    blue, pink, turquoise and orange
Fabric glue
Tracing paper
Colored pencils or tailor's chalk
Pinking shears

Nativity scene tree skirt

Black soutache braid edges the figures and combines with the white background to give this brightly colored Nativity scene a glowing vibrancy, like a stained glass window lit from behind. All the figures from the familiar story are there – the shepherds, the wise men, the donkey, the ox and lambs, Mary, Joseph and Jesus, with the star above them.

Children will love these simple outline figures bearing the Christmas message, and the tree skirt is not difficult to make. The entire scene, including the soutache braid and even the red and green braid around the top and bottom of the circle, is pressed and glued in place, so there is no sewing involved at all. To complete the effect, cut out similar motifs from colored cardboard for tree decorations.

Cutting out

First draw a grid of 1in squares on tracing paper and copy all the figures, square by square, onto the tracing paper grid, thus enlarging them to the full size. Do not cut out the shapes from tracing paper at this stage, but number each separate part that will have to be cut from felt: for example, the cradle (1), the coverlet (2), the face (3), the halo (4), Joseph's habit (5), headgear (6), face (7), hand (8) and staff (9). Note that in some cases, such as Joseph's headgear, the braid lies over a solid piece of one color.

When you have numbered each piece on the enlarged figures, make a tracing of the finished design, as shown, and write the corresponding numbers on this tracing, as a guide when you position the pieces.

Cut out the numbered pieces of the enlarged drawings and, using the photograph of the finished design as a color guide, use them as pattern pieces to mark the outlines on the felt. Hold each paper pattern against the felt and carefully mark the outline with a colored pencil or tailor's chalk. Cut out the felt shapes and either number them on the back or lightly pin each piece to its numbered pattern piece. Try to keep the pieces needed for each figure together – if space is limited and you must pile the pieces up, put a sheet of paper between each figure and the next.

If the felt is very thin, fuse the felt to fusible interfacing before cutting out the pieces.

Cut out the shape of the tree skirt as described for the skirt on page 54, but do not scallop the edges. Use pinking shears to cut around both the outer and the inner circles, then use ordinary dressmaking shears to cut straight up from the outer circle to the inner circle. If the felt is too thin, fuse it to fusible interfacing before cutting out the skirt.

Assembling the skirt

Lay the white background flat and assemble the figures in position on the background, following the photograph overleaf and positioning each figure 7in up from the outer edge. Pin each piece in position. You will find that it is easiest to start with the cradle at the center front and then work outward to each side.

When all the pieces are in position, glue them in place, making sure that all joining edges neatly butt up against each other.

Use the photograph as a guide for positioning the Nativity figures beginning with the cradle and working outward at each side.

For matching tree decorations, simply trace the main outlines given and transfer to black paper.

Cut out the individual pieces of the tracings – to be used as patterns for cutting out the different details from colored paper. Follow the directions given for making the felt figures but instead of using black braid for the outline, allow the black paper to show between the shapes. Make hanging loops using a needle and fine gold thread.

Starting with all the shorter lengths, glue the braid in position, covering all joins and using it to draw in any details, such as the shape of Joseph's sleeve. Finish by taking soutache braid all around the outline of each figure.

It is important to prevent the glue from smearing the right side of the figures. Use a glue gun if you have one, or use a knitting needle or similar tool to spread a light coating of glue carefully on the back of the braid.

The tight curves are the most difficult sections to work. It will help if you stick pins through the soutache braid and into the felt, standing the pins upright, as if they were on a pincushion, to hold the shape until the glue has set.

When the figures are completed, apply the wool braid to both the inner and outer edges in the same way, again using upright pins to hold it while the glue is setting. Begin by placing the red braid with the lower edge 1½in up from the outer edge of the skirt, folding the ends under to the wrong side at the slit edge. Repeat the process to put a second circle of red braid 1½in down from the inner edge. Apply the green braid in the same way, positioning it 1in inside the braid at the lower edge and ¾in at the top edge.

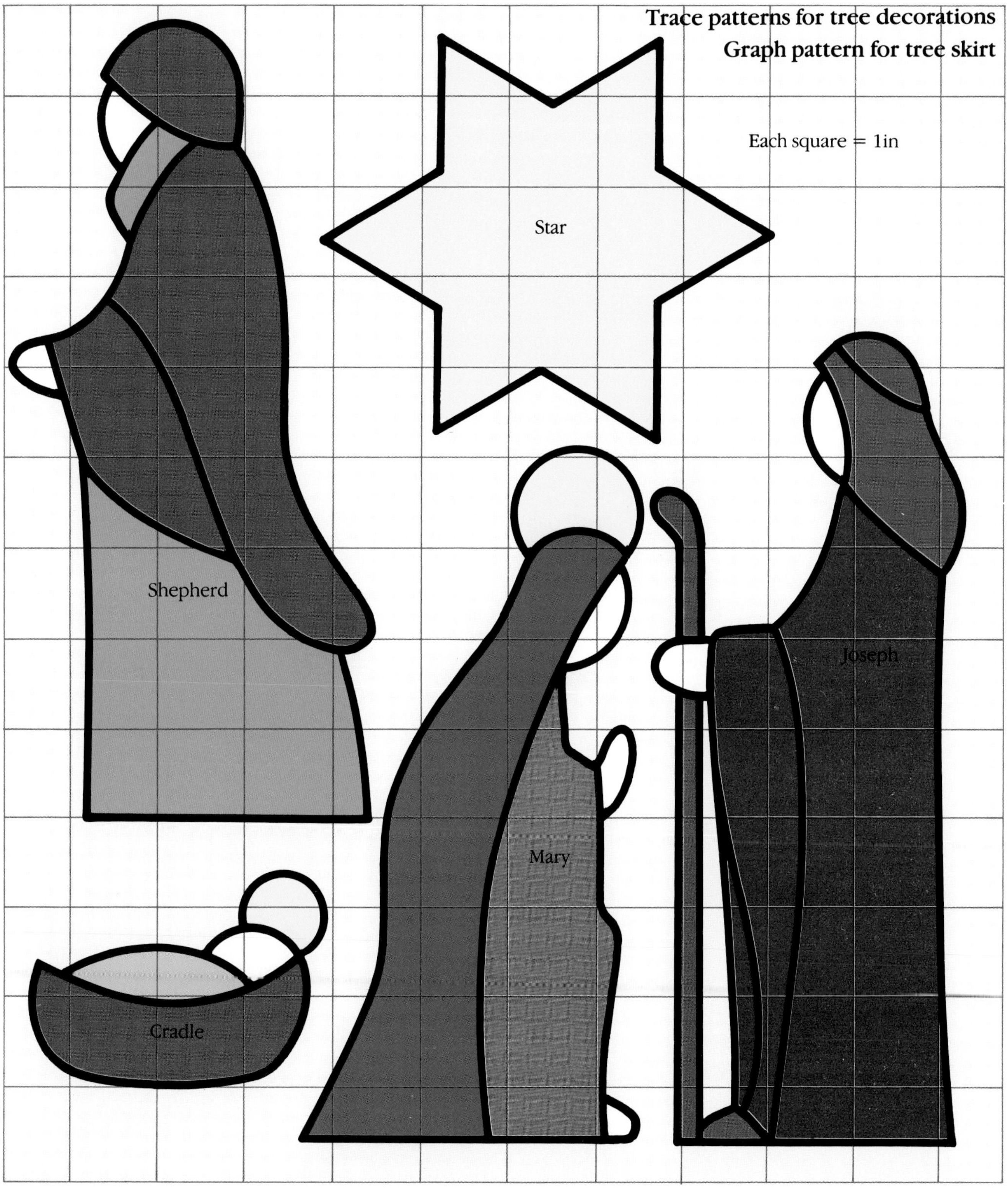

Trace patterns for tree decorations
Graph pattern for tree skirt

Each square = 1in

Star

Shepherd

Joseph

Mary

Cradle

Each square = 1in

Ass

King

Sheep

King

Ox

Shepherd

King

CHAPTER 3

We wish you a merry Christmas

The custom of sending Christmas cards was a Victorian invention, a practice which took shape in the mid 19th century (the original inventor is a matter of dispute) and rapidly became part of the Christmas tradition; for what better way is there, in a busy world, of reminding faraway friends and relatives that they are not forgotten? These charming hand-made cards make the point more clearly than any commercial offering. In addition to a selection of different cards, there is a beautiful advent calendar, hand-printed paper, and a set of boxes which would surely be almost as welcome as the presents inside them.

Advent calendar

This glowing advent calendar is based on the idea of a stained-glass triptych window with sunlight pouring through. The construction is not in itself difficult; the main requirement is time and patience in cutting the 24 silhouette pictures that make up this highly unusual and effective calendar.

Cutting out

First cut out the basic triptych outline of the calendar from black and blue cardboard or poster board. Working first on the black, draw on the back a grid of 1in squares and copy the shaped outline of the top, square by square, from the graph pattern given on pages 68-69. Mark the windows in position on the back. When the outline and window details are marked, cut along the outline and remove the windows from the blue cardboard.

Place the blue calendar outline on the back of the black cardboard and, using it as a pattern, mark the outline and the outlines of the windows on the black cardboard. Cut out the main outline on the black cardboard, and working from the back, cut out the window shutters: cut along the bottom sill of each window; cut down the center from the point of the arch straight down to the sill, then cut the curved sides of the arch, leaving the straight sides uncut, to form the hinges. Using the blunt edge of a knife or a knitting needle, carefully score along the foldline at each hinge. Fold each shutter back and crease it carefully, then fold it back flat.

Using the same method of creasing and folding, make folds between the three arched panels of the calendar on both pieces of cardboard. Make sure that the folds lie in exactly the same place on the black and blue cardboard, and fold them so that the black front of the calendar will stand as shown in the picture, and with the blue cardboard at the back, wrong sides together.

Silhouettes

On the remaining black cardboard, draw 19 rectangles measuring 4in x 2¾in, four measuring 2¾in x 2in and one measuring 5½in x 4¾in, and cut these out. Cut pieces of tracing paper to the same sizes, then carefully trace over the silhouette outlines given for the windows. Attach each tracing to the appropriate piece of cardboard using small pieces of masking tape, leaving an even amount of frame around the edge.

Cutting through both the tracing paper and cardboard, carefully cut out each silhouette, using an X-acto knife. You may find it easier to tape the cardboard to a small piece of fiberboard, so that you can turn the cardboard around as you cut. Cut out the stars above the center panel.

Assembling the calendar

Take the black calendar shape and lay it on a flat surface, wrong side up, then, following the key on pages 68-69, lightly glue the silhouettes in place. Only a little glue is needed – at the appropriate outer points and the bottom edges of each silhouette – and care must be taken to position the shapes so that they fall exactly in place at the correct window.

When all the silhouettes have been attached to the black calendar section, cut out rectangles of tissue paper the right size and in the color of your choice. Put a thin layer of glue around the edges of the windows and arrange the colors to create the stained glass effect, as seen in the photograph. Next, put a layer of glue all around the outside edge and along the edges between the arches, ready to stick the black and blue sections together. Lay the black calendar wrong (inside) side down on top of the blue one. Don't get any glue on the shutters.

To keep the shutters closed, use gold star stickers, and if you wish, mark each star with the relevant opening date, numbering them from one to 24, using the number stickers.

Materials

Two sheets each of black and blue thin cardboard measuring 30¾in x 20½in
A selection of bright blue, green, yellow, orange, red and purple tissue papers
Tracing paper and pencil
X-acto knife
Metal ruler
Clear glue
Gold star stickers
Number stickers 1-24 (optional)

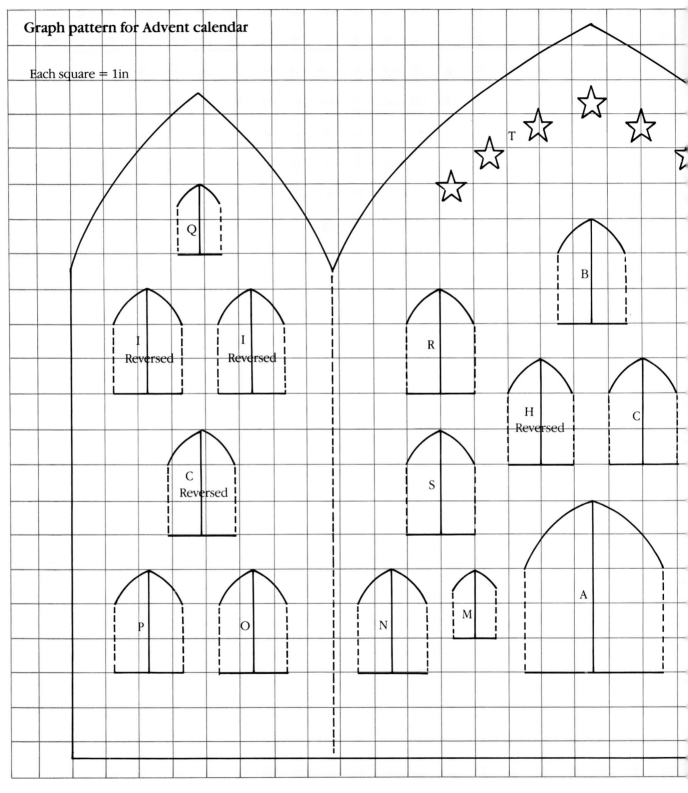

Graph pattern for Advent calendar

Each square = 1in

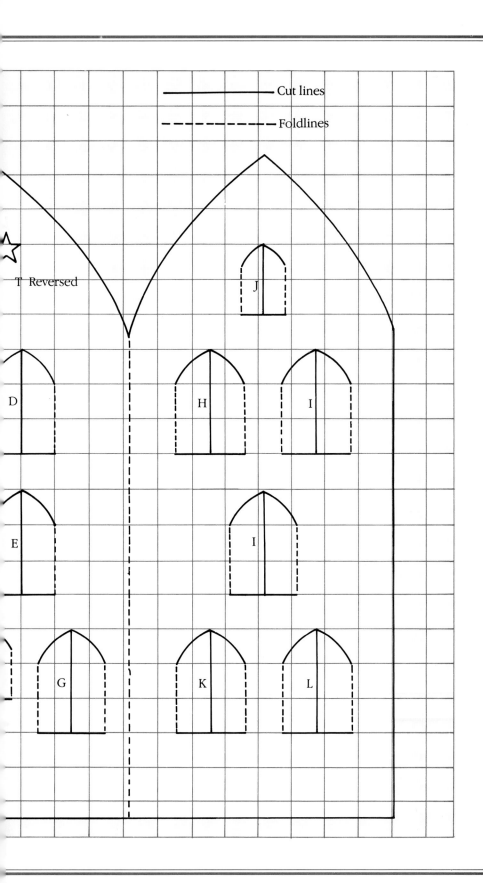

Cut lines

Foldlines

T Reversed

J

D

H

I

E

I

G

K

L

Trace patterns for silhouettes

Window outline

Q

Window outline

B

Window outline

J

A

Trace patterns for silhouettes

Window outline

D

Window outline

R

O

P

N

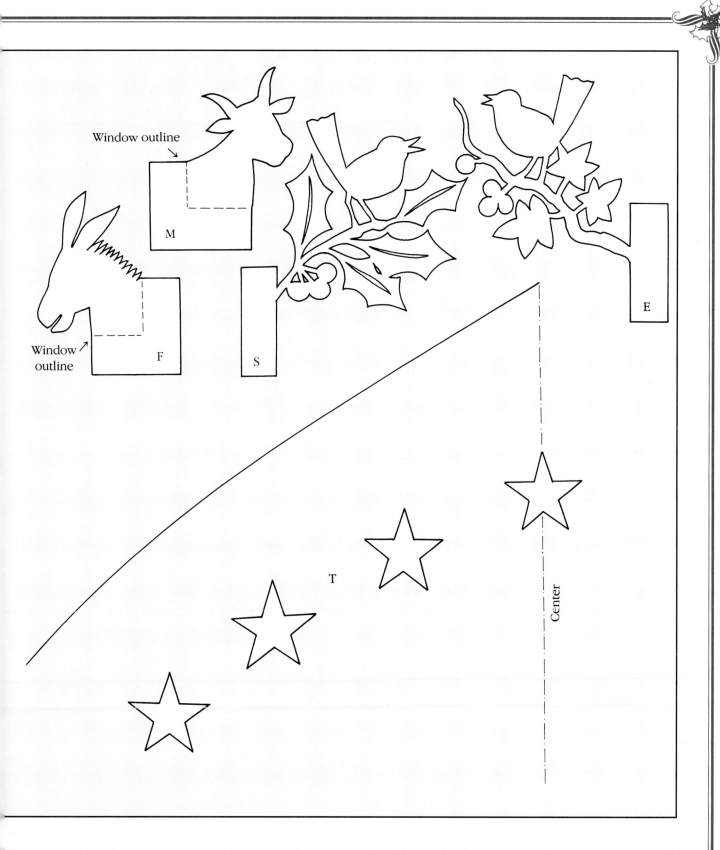

Window outline

M

Window
outline

F

S

E

T

Center

Materials

13¼in x 8in pieces of lightweight red
    cardboard
6½in x 5½in piece of white poster
    board
Tracing paper and pencil
X-acto knife
Clear glue

Partridge in a pear tree

In essence, this delicate silhouette
card is simplicity itself to make – all
that is needed is to take care with the
cutting, particularly around the white
frame area where the positive image
turns to a negative one. You can make
the card in a silhouette form as here,
where the white cut-out is simply set
behind an open frame or, if you wish
to make several cards, you could cut

the design as a stencil and use this to
color as many cards as you need.

Making the card

First trace the design. Go over the
outline on the wrong side and then
transfer it to the poster board,
centering it so that there is a margin of
at least ⅜in all around beyond the
outer white frame.

    Carefully cut out the design as
shown in the photograph, making

Trace pattern for silhouette and border

sure that you leave enough paper to link areas, such as the grass at the side of the picture, the details on the bird or the fallen pears, where the image changes from positive to negative.

Fold the colored cardboard in half to make a card measuring 8in x 6⅝in, with the fold at the top edge. For the frame, cut out a window measuring 5½in x 4¾in from the front. Put glue at the back of the frame, around the edges, then gently position the silhouette over the back of the frame and press it in place.

Stenciling

If you wish to make a stencil in order to produce several cards, you must first copy the design on stencil board, available from art supply stores. Trace the design and then use carbon paper to transfer the design to the board. Cut the design out carefully and use the stencil to color the background (cut out) areas either directly on the cardboard or on white poster board which can be framed in the same way as the silhouette. Use a single color or several to vary the effect.

Pop-up Santa Claus

If you own a pop-up book or have browsed through samples in book stores you will realize that some of the mechanisms involved can be very complex. When money is no object, it is even possible to create a fully formed galleon, with each plank and every piece of rigging and sail rising into place as the book is opened and then, incredibly, all folding away once again. But before you close this book in alarm, our pop-up is very easy to make, even though it has all the impact of the unexpected as Santa Claus leaps up like a jack-in-the-box when you open the card. Write your Christmas message on the back of the card, or print it on a small label and attach it to one of his hands.

Cutting out

Fold the blue cardboard in half to make a card measuring 6in x 4¼in, trimming the edges to even them up if necessary.

Trace over the outlines for the body, the head and the movement (two sections, one with tabs C, D, E and F and one with E and F marked at the top edge). Transfer the outlines to the red cardboard. Transfer the outline for the face to pink paper and cut it out, leaving the nose to be cut later. Transfer the outlines for the pompon, hands, hat trim and beard to white paper and cut out. Next, cut out the mouth.

Glue the pink face and the white details in place on the red cardboard outlines, then carefully cut out, making a slit as marked at the bottom of the nose. Stick on the eyes.

Assembling the card

Using the back of a knife or a knitting needle, run along the foldlines – marked with dashes – of the head, body and movement. Carefully fold along these scored lines: fold the face in half, right side inside, then push the nose the other way, so that the nose

stands out when the face is opened.

Fold tabs A and B forward to the front of the body and fold the body down the center, right side inside.

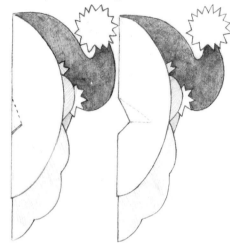

Fold at the wrists to give a little more shape to the completed card, then bring the hands up in line with the body. Glue tabs A and B in position at the top of the forehead (marked with dotted lines A and B).

Glue tabs E and F to the card so that the dashed foldlines lie along the dotted placement lines, with the tabs below the placement lines and the movement above. Glue the second movement section so that it covers tabs E and F and the bottom edge lies on the bottom edge of the card. Fold the tabbed section down so that when the card is closed the central foldline lies below placement lines E-F and tabs C and D are folded upward.

Glue tabs C and D, facing upward, to the back of the body along placement lines C and D.

When assembling the pieces, take care to allow the glue to dry thoroughly at each stage before you move on to the next, otherwise they may slip and prevent the card from folding. Take great care also not to tear the pieces.

Write your message on the back or front of the card, or on a separate label, as suggested. Attach it to the hand using a small dot of glue.

Materials

8½in x 6in piece of medium-weight blue cardboard
11in x 8in piece of thin red cardboard or poster board
8in square of white paper
3in square of pink paper
Two round blue stickers
Tracing paper and pencil
X-acto knife
Clear glue

Trace patterns for Santa Claus

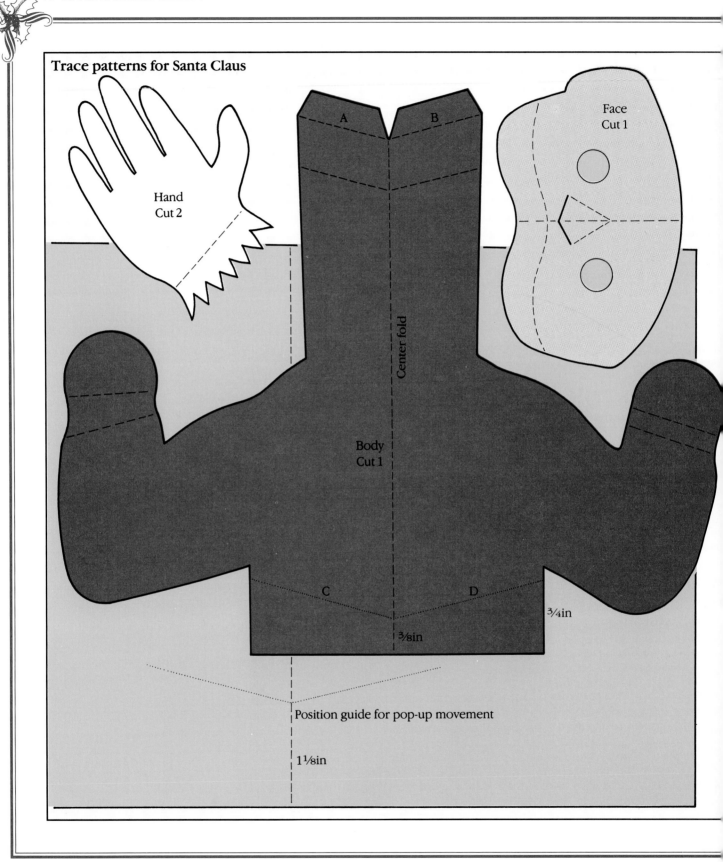

Hand
Cut 2

Face
Cut 1

A   B

Center fold

Body
Cut 1

C   D

³/₄in

³/₈in

Position guide for pop-up movement

1¹/₈in

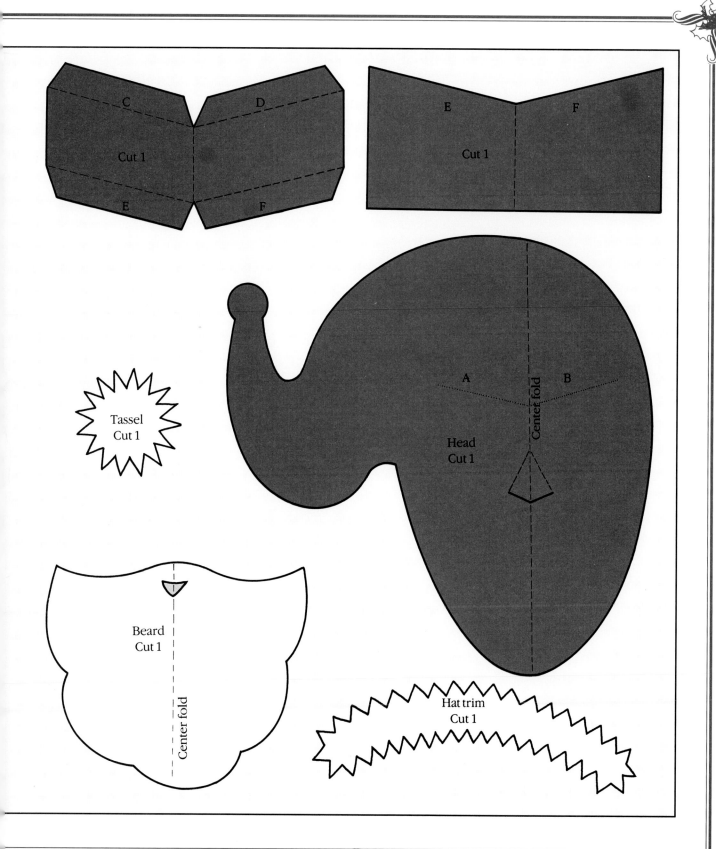

Cut 1

C   D

E   F

E   F

Cut 1

Tassel
Cut 1

A   B

Center fold

Head
Cut 1

Beard
Cut 1

Center fold

Hat trim
Cut 1

Materials

Medium-thick cardboard – approximately
    20in x 8in
Thin cardboard cut into ¼in-wide strips
    – two strips 4¾in long and one strip
    8in long
10in squares of fabric – one of red
    cotton, one of pale yellow cotton,
    and one of backing fabric
Batting
Light green, medium green, red and
    dark brown cotton embroidery floss
Variegated silk thread
Silver Lurex thread
Red, yellow and light gray sewing
    thread
Fabric glue
8in-wide embroidery hoop
Metal ruler
X-acto knife

Embroidered card

If you enjoy embroidery, here is a
delightful card for someone you are
fond of and for whom you want to
take a bit more time and trouble. The
finished card measures 8in x 5½in
and will fit into an envelope
measuring 8½in x 6⅛in.

Making the mount

From the medium cardboard, cut one
piece measuring 8in x 5½in for the
cardboard mount. Cut out the window
as shown on the pattern and cut the
small label from the inner square.
Draw a red line around the label and
punch or cut a hole at the mitered
end.

Trim the remaining medium
cardboard to a rectangle, fold it in half
and cut it to measure 11in x 8in
(unfolded).

Draw the outside shape of the
mount pattern on the red fabric, then
place it in an embroidery hoop and,
using light green, medium green and
red embroidery floss, satin stitch the
holly leaves and berries as shown.
Finish each berry with a brown
French knot. Take the fabric from the
hoop; press, then cut out the outer
shape but not the inner square,
leaving a ½in seam allowance all
around. Place the fabric right side
down on the table, then lay the
cardboard mount on top, making sure
that the motif is at the bottom.

Fold the raw edges of the fabric
over the cardboard and glue them
down. Cut out the center square
leaving at least ⅝in of fabric for
turning under; miter the corners as
indicated on the pattern. Fold the raw
edges back over the cardboard and
glue them down.

Using the variegated thread, make a
twisted cord long enough to run
around the inner edge of the square,
with enough left over to make a tie for
the label. Take as many strands as you
need to achieve the necessary
thickness when twisted as follows. Cut

the strands three times the length of
the finished cord, place them together
and knot each end. Fasten one end of
the cord around a door handle and,
holding the strands taut, insert a
pencil through the knotted end and
rotate them until they are tightly
twisted. Remove the pencil, fold the
twisted cord in half at the center and
knot the ends together. Holding the
knot, give a sharp shake to the cord
and even out the twists by smoothing
them, starting from the knotted end.
Tie another knot at the fold to hold
the twists.

Slip stitch the cord around the inner
square, keeping the remaining piece
for the tie.

Making the present

To transfer the pattern for the present
to the center of the yellow cotton, first
trace over the design, then lay the
fabric right side up on a flat surface.
Hold the fabric to the surface with
strips of masking tape at the corners.
Again taping the corners, place the
tracing over the fabric, then slip
dressmaker's carbon paper, carbon
side down, between the tracing paper
and the fabric. Mark the lines of the
design with a pencil or a tracing
wheel.

Place the marked fabric in the
embroidery hoop and satin stitch the
holly and berries. Using gray thread,
couch the silver thread in swirls and
loops over and around the motifs.
Remove the fabric from the ring and
press it with a warm iron on the
wrong side, then cut out the fabric and
batting pieces.

Place batting under each of the
flaps, turn down the top corner and
then the matching sides and make a
neat backstitch to hold the corner. Pin
the batting and fabric together.

Place the backing fabric in the
embroidery hoop and pin the
rectangular piece in the center.
Backstitch along the stitching line as
indicated (this will be the inner fold of
the small pleat across the present).

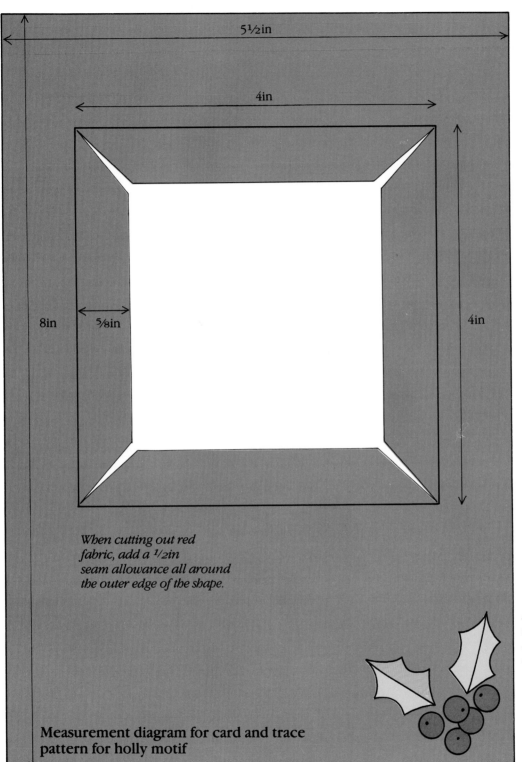

5½in

4in

8in   ⅝in

4in

When cutting out red fabric, add a ¹/₂in seam allowance all around the outer edge of the shape.

Measurement diagram for card and trace pattern for holly motif

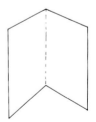

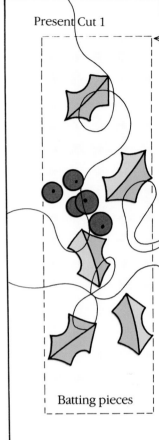

Present Cut 1

Batting pieces

Medium-weight cardboard measuring 11in x 8in scored and folded along center line

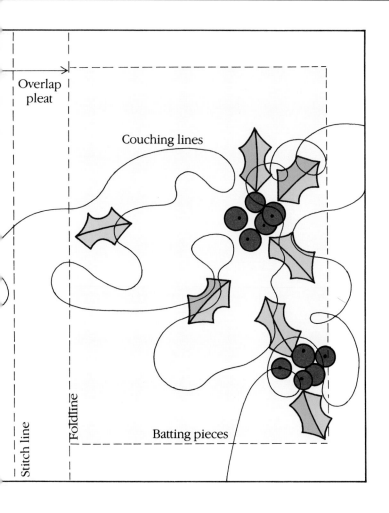

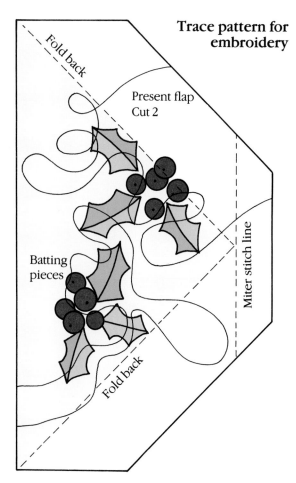

Trace pattern for embroidery

Present flap
Cut 2

Trace pattern for label

Remove the pins and put batting under the bottom half, then pin again. Bring the two foldlines together and insert the batting for the top half of the rectangle, and pin. The batting will raise the fabric, slightly decreasing the finished size.

Pin the flaps in position so that they lie over the square section, with raw edges matching at either side. Before sewing around the edge of the present to hold the pieces together, place the mount over the work to check that it will fit and that none of the stitches will be visible.

Wrap variegated thread around the strips of cardboard, gluing the ends to keep the threads in place. Use the two shorter lengths to make a cross shape

over the present, then make an unknotted bow shape with the longer length by twisting the two ends around and crossing them at the center. Place the "bow" at the center of the cross and make a few stitches with variegated thread to hold the bow together. Remove from the hoop and trim the edges to within ⅝in.

Assembling the card
On the back of the cardboard mount, glue around the edge of the center square. Place the mount carefully over the present and over the front of the folded card, making sure that the fold is on the left. Tie on the label for writing a name or a short greeting so that it hangs just below the present.

Materials

10in square of 18-mesh-to-the-inch mono canvas

12in x 6in piece of medium-thick cardboard

6in square of thin cardboard

DMC six-stranded cotton embroidery floss as follows: one skein each of red #606, cherry #600, greens #943 and #702, and white; two skeins each of blue #809 and pale gray #3024, and three skeins each of cream #746 and browns #400 and #801

One ball of lightweight gold metallic yarn

Size #20 tapestry needle

Sequin stars

Invisible sewing thread

Metal ruler

X-acto knife

Continental stitch (diagonal)

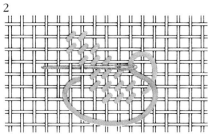

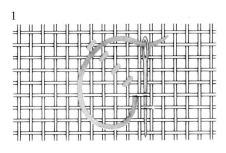

Plum pudding card

This charming needlepoint card, worked in stranded embroidery floss on fine canvas, features a traditional plum pudding with its cheerful, rounded shape. A card as delightful as this is definitely more of a keepsake than just a card, so this is carefully mounted, ready for display on successive years.

Preparing the canvas

Cover the edges of the canvas with masking tape to prevent them from raveling.

Trace over the outlines of the design and transfer it to the center of the canvas either with dressmaker's carbon paper (see page 80) or in the following way.

First trace the design and transfer it to poster board. Strengthen the outlines with a black felt-tipped pen.

Place the canvas in the center of the design, lining up the right-angles of the canvas mesh with the right-angles of the outer square. Hold the canvas and paper firmly in position with thumb tacks or masking tape, so that they cannot slip.

Shine an adjustable lamp at an angle toward the canvas so that the design outlines show through, then copy the design onto the canvas with a waterproof marker.

Ideally the canvas should be embroidered in a frame to keep it evenly stretched, but you can manage without a frame if you do not have one. Simply remember not to pull the stitching too tightly.

Continental stitch (diagonal)

Work with six strands of thread in the needle (the gold yarn is worked in single strands) using continental stitch and working in diagonal rows wherever possible. It is best to work diagonally because the horizontal and vertical stitches at the back of the work help to prevent the canvas from becoming distorted. To work diagonal rows, bring the needle through to the front of the canvas and insert it to the right of the intersection of threads above. Take the needle behind two horizontal threads of canvas so that it emerges at the bottom of the next stitch (1).

Work the first row from top left to bottom right and the second from bottom right to top left. Bring out the needle at the bottom of the stitch, insert it to the right of the intersection of threads above and take it horizontally behind two vertical threads, ready for the next stitch (2).

Working the needlepoint

Work from the center of the design outward, starting with the pudding. The danger is that the cream could get dirty so take great care to avoid this. Work small areas, such as the dots in the pudding, first.

Scatter white spots in the sky (single stitches) to give the effect of snow. These are placed at random, but at the same time care is needed to keep them evenly distributed.

The inner border is worked with two rows of gold metallic yarn, as is the plate border. For the outer border, start at one corner and work around the frame, alternating two rows of gray #3024 with five rows of cream #746. Make sure that the stripes are consistent where they appear to pass behind the central picture.

When the picture is finished sew on the sequin stars, again starting from one corner and making sure that they are evenly scattered around the border. Use invisible thread to sew them in position.

Mounting

Score the large piece of cardboard across the center with an X-acto knife so it will fold neatly into two squares.

Measure the finished needlepoint picture to check the size (approximately 5in square). Lay the cardboard flat and cut out a window to

Trace pattern for plum pudding card

Key

A	White	F	Cherry #600
B	Cream	G	Red #606
C	Blue #809	H	Pale gray #3024
D	Green #702	I	Brown #400
E	Green #943	J	Dark brown #801
		K	Gold metallic yarn

this measurement on one (front) side, leaving an equal border all around.

Trim the edges of the canvas, still leaving a margin of unworked canvas all around the picture. Place it behind the cardboard window and secure it with masking tape. The finished card stands on an A-shaped base, so the fold in the card comes at the top of the frame and gold cord forms the cross stroke of the A-shape.

Thread gold metallic yarn into a sewing needle and push the needle through the thin cardboard to make a hole ¾in up from one edge (now the lower edge) and centered. Take the needle through the corresponding point at the back of the cardboard frame. Knot the cord at both ends to make a support 3in long between the two pieces of cardboard.

Position the thin cardboard to cover the back of the needlepoint picture and glue it around the edges.

Collage snow scenes

Fabric collage cards are easy to make and can be extremely effective, and although they look as if each one has taken a great deal of time and individual attention in the making, they are in fact relatively simple to mass-produce. A raid on your fabric drawer will probably bring to light plenty of suitable odds and ends, or you may have scraps of fabric from other Christmas projects; the rest is a gentle exercise of your ingenuity and imagination. If you do not enjoy sewing, there is no need to stitch the strips together – they can just be fused to a base. Finishing touches can be either drawn in with waterproof inks, cut out from felt and stuck to the background or embroidered – the choice is yours.

Materials

Snowman card

Scraps of unbleached muslin (first fabric), panne velvet, corduroy or satin (second fabric), and Christmas fabric (third fabric)

4in x 2½in piece of medium-weight fusible interfacing

Permanent markers in red and black (if you do not have permanent markers, you may be able to use felt-tipped pens but check first on a scrap of fabric to make sure that the inks do not run)

Pink and blue sprays (you could use watercolors and a paintbrush if you prefer)

Small quantity of green and red embroidery floss

Pale green sewing thread

Multi-purpose (fabric/paper) glue

12in x 6in piece of thin cardboard

Metal ruler and X-acto knife

Snow scene card

Scraps of cotton with white polkadots (first fabric), white felt (second fabric), and silver satin or Lurex fabric (third fabric), also green felt for trees

6¼in x 3¾in piece of medium-weight fusible interfacing

White sewing thread

Multi-purpose (fabric/paper) glue

14¼in x 4½in piece of thin cardboard and the same quantity of poster board

Snowman card

Cut the unbleached muslin to measure 2½in x 1¾in then lightly spray or paint it with pink and blue, as shown on the photograph. Using the permanent marker draw the snowman freehand at the center of the fabric piece and fill in details. You may find it easier to draw in pencil first then go over the lines with the marker.

Lay the fusible interfacing shiny side up on an ironing board and place the unbleached muslin over it, right side up, matching the top edge of the muslin with the top edge of the interfacing.

Cut the second fabric to measure 2½in x 1⅛in and lay it over the interfacing so that the top edge of the second fabric overlaps the bottom edge of the muslin by ¼in.

Cut the third fabric to measure 2½in x 1⅜in and lay it in position, with the bottom edge of the fabric matching the bottom edge of the fusible interfacing.

Following the manufacturer's instructions, fuse the pieces of fabric to the interfacing.

With pale green thread and an open machine zigzag stitch, sew along the two raw edges of adjoining pieces of fabric.

Using straight stitch and green embroidery floss, embroider the stems of the flowers, then make the red flowers with French knots (the flowers can be stitched by machine, using ordinary sewing threads, if preferred).

Neatly fold the cardboard into thirds, bringing one (right-hand) section to the front of the central section and one (left-hand) section to the back. From the section that now lies on the front of the card, cut out a window measuring 3½in x 2in.

Lay the card unfolded, with the front window section right side down, on your work surface. Put a layer of glue around the edges of the center section and carefully lay the collage, right side up, over it. Put glue around the wrong side of the front frame and bring it over the collage.

Snow scene card

Trim the white polkadot fabric to measure 6¼in x 3¾in and fuse it to the interfacing. Next cut the white felt into a strip 6¼in wide and 2⅛in deep. Cut one long (top) edge in a curved shape, then glue it to the background, matching the long straight edge with the bottom edge of the background.

Cut the silver fabric into a strip 6¼in wide and 1½in deep, then shape it in the same way and glue it to the background. Applying the fabrics in layers like this will give a slight impression of relief to the picture, so that the final strip will appear to lie more in the foreground.

Stitch along the edges between the strips with an open machine zigzag stitch and white thread. Finally cut out

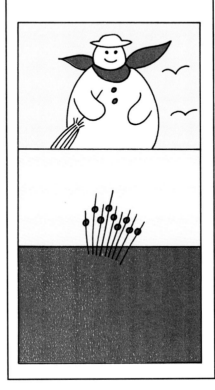

Trace pattern for snowman

two Christmas trees from green felt, one slightly smaller than the other. Glue the smaller tree in position, then the larger tree, positioning the latter so that it just overlaps the smaller tree at one corner.

Fold the cardboard in half neatly, then from the front of the cardboard cut out a window measuring 6in x 3¼in. Glue around the edges of the frame, on the wrong side, then carefully press the collage in position, so that it is framed by the cardboard. Fold the poster board, trimming it if necessary, and glue it to the inside of the card, neatly covering the back of the collage. This method can enable you to reuse an old card, assuming that the original card was framed around a picture: all you need to do is to cut out the original scene, insert your collage, then cover the inside with poster board.

Mass-producing cards

Cards of this type can easily be mass-produced. All you need do is to cut

your strips across the entire width of the fabric, and join them together with zigzag stitching in the same way as for individual cards. Add the details at regular intervals: for example, for the snowman card you would draw a snowman every 2½in to make 13 cards from 36in-wide fabric.

If you layer the strips on a background fabric, as described for the snow scene, you do not necessarily need to use fusible interfacing, although it will make stitching and cutting easier.

Certain fabrics lend themselves particularly well to landscape collages of this type. The fabrics used in the snow scene are obvious examples, but others are equally suitable: brown corduroy can give the impression of ploughed fields in winter; black, dark blue or green velvets can be used for hills at night; and pale pink or peach satins can provide dawn or sunset skies. Use nets and polkadotted sheers to suggest snowy effects and Lurex fabrics to add festive sparkle.

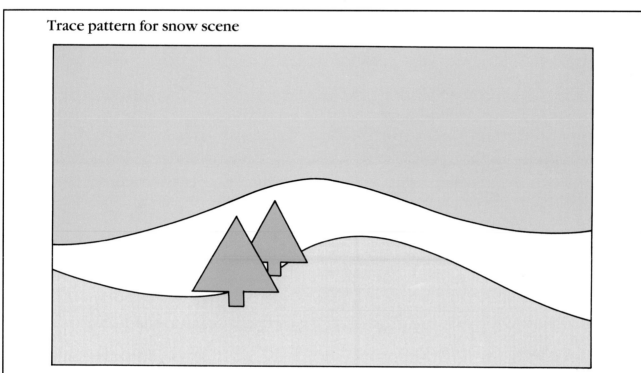

Trace pattern for snow scene

Hand-printed paper

The perfect finishing touch to a delightful, handmade gift is an exclusive wrapping paper, designed and hand-printed in the home. Linocuts are derived from woodcuts, the chief advantage being that linocuts are much easier to do. The design is made by cutting away the unwanted portions of the linoleum surface, inking what remains, and pressing the lino block down on the paper so that the inked portions print the image.

This pretty Christmas paper would make a good project for children, but they should be at least ten years old, as linocutting blades are very sharp. The technique is divided into several separate stages – design, making the blocks, preparing the paper and printing – so they need not complete it in one session, and they can enjoy learning about this very simple and traditional form of printing as they work.

The equipment needed for making linocuts and the inks are available from art and craft stores, including the linoleum itself, which must be the old-fashioned, canvas-backed and matte-finished type, not the vinyl flooring that is commonly used today.

Design

You can use any of the designs shown here, or you might prefer to choose your own Christmas motif. Perhaps you might like to combine a Christmas symbol with your own monogram, to give your gifts a highly individual stamp. Children can also be encouraged to experiment with their own designs.

The printed design is made by the areas which remain after the background has been cut away, so to make the motifs shown here, it is necessary to cut away everything but the outlines. This means that the blocks are relatively difficult to make, but printing is much easier than it would be if larger areas remained. An alternative way of making the tree image, for instance, would be to cut away only the areas of the lino block outside the tree and the tub, along with the decorations and the inside of the star, and to leave the rest of the tree and tub. You would then have a solid image instead of an outline, and there would be less cutting involved, but you might have problems in keeping the image clean and neat when printing.

If you are designing your own motifs, therefore, it is best to keep the outlines clear and uncomplicated. It would be irritating to spoil a sheet of wrapping paper covered with several repeated images by having one or two not entirely successful motifs. If you enjoy making linocuts and wish to experiment with a more detailed picture or design, you could try making a Christmas card as described on page 94, in which case any blurred or unsuccessful prints could be thrown away.

When you have chosen your motifs, carefully copy each one onto trace-down paper.

Making the blocks

The first stage is to cut your linoleum into appropriately sized blocks. Decide how far apart you wish to space your images and then cut your blocks to a size that will give you this spacing when printing (see Printing on page 93) and that will easily contain the motif.

The easiest way to cut the linoleum to the required size is to mark the outer measurements of the block on the back and then cut through the burlap with an X-acto knife. After this you should be able to crack the linoleum apart.

Before you start making a block, experiment with your cutting tool and practice making lines with the various blades. The blades are very sharp, so when you are cutting try to keep the hand that is holding the block behind the cutting hand as much as possible.

Materials

Linoleum – amount according to the size of the motifs and number of blocks to be used

Paper – either fine white paper with a lightly glazed finish (the glaze must not be heavy or the ink will run – obtainable from art supply stores), or lightweight lining paper

Water-based block printing inks in the chosen colors (it is preferable to buy water-based inks as these can be cleaned up with water)

Trace-down paper (like carbon paper, but made for designers and available at art supply stores – any unwanted marks are more easily removed than ordinary carbon paper lines)

X-acto knife

Linocutting tool with wide and narrow V-shaped and broad U-shaped blades

Wood blocks or empty thread spools (to back the lino blocks)

PVA glue

Roller for printing

Slab on which to roll out the inks – a sheet of glass or fiberboard will serve the purpose

Pencil

Long ruler

Eraser

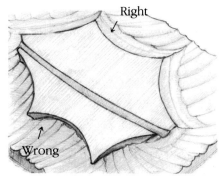

Hold the ball of the handle against your palm and guide the tool with your thumb and forefinger, with the U or V turned upward. Push the tool gently forward to make a groove. (If you dig in too deeply or at too sharp an angle you are likely to make mistakes or your hand could slip.) By turning the block slowly as you work you will be able to make a curved line. You will probably find it easiest to work in fairly short lines, removing the loose linoleum as you cut.

The narrow V-shaped blade is used to run the initial cuts along each side of the final printed (raised) outlines, and you can then move to the wider V-shape, using the broad U-shape for removing large areas.

The sides of the cuts should slope outward as shown in the diagram, so that the printing surface of the block remains firm. If your grooves slope inward or are too steep-sided, the printing surface will be undermined.

When you have experimented with cutting and have mastered the technique, prepare your blocks. Using the tracings of your chosen designs, lay each block on a flat surface with the trace-down paper over the smooth side and trace over the design. With the narrow V-shaped blade, start by cutting away on either side of the lines, as already described. Remember that the remaining portion, in

Trace patterns for motifs

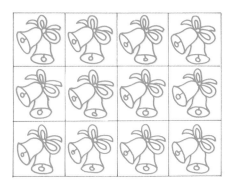

between the two cutting lines, will be the part that prints, so try to keep this an even width.

When you have cut away all the linoleum surface apart from the design outlines, carefully brush and dust the blocks to make sure that there are no loose pieces left. These have an annoying tendency to stick to the inked roller and spoil prints, so it is essential to tidy up before you move to the next stage.

Glue either a small wood block or a spool firmly to the back of each block – you can then hold the block more easily when printing and it is less likely to smear the paper.

Printing

The first essential when printing is to make sure that you have plenty of space. (Other activities do not mix with printing, which is another reason why it is a good idea if all the family can join in.) You will need an area to print and also a space where wet prints can be laid out to dry.

Spread old newspaper (the ink from new newspaper tends to leave marks) or an old cloth over your working surface.

Start by preparing your paper for printing. Measure the block that you are using to print any particular sheet of paper and divide the sheet up into squares or rectangles with these measurements, using your pencil and the long ruler, and marking the paper as lightly as possible, as shown opposite.

Squeeze a line of ink the length of your roller onto the board. Roll this out, rolling in several directions to make sure it's evenly distributed. Do not use too much at a time – a good test is that the ink should make a sticky noise when you roll it. Check again that there are no loose pieces of linoleum on your block and that the ink covers the roller evenly.

Roll ink from the slab onto the raised surface of the linoleum block, again rolling in different directions to make sure it is evenly covered (recharging the roller if necessary).

The layer of ink should be very thin. If it is too thick, the ink will spread and the print will be spoiled. Before starting on a sheet of paper, check on a small scrap that the image is as you want it: if necessary, clean the block and cut away any unwanted pieces.

Repeat patterns

To print, simply press the block firmly down on the paper, using the ruled lines as a guide to help you to get your print in the right position.

You can print all in one color or use different colors. If you are using several colors, for example alternating green and red bells, complete all the motifs in one color first before changing to the second color. In between colors, wash and dry the slab and the roller and remove all traces of the previous color from the block.

In addition to wrapping paper you can also make strips of paper ribbon by repeating tiny motifs in the same way.

When you have finished printing, leave the paper for a few days to dry out. This may be a nuisance, but the ink is slow-drying so patience is the best policy.

When the ink is completely dry, carefully erase the pencil lines.

Other ideas

If you enjoy making linocuts, you will find that it can be used in many different ways for Christmas gifts and notions.

You may like to make linocut Christmas cards. Start by drawing the design. Assuming that the design is likely to be more complex than the simple image repeats used for wrapping paper, you will probably find it easier to cut out the outlines and the details, in which case the background will be solid color while the original color of the paper will show through at the design lines.

If you do not feel very inspired as an artist, try tracing over an old Christmas card or a drawing from an old book, simplifying the lines as necessary to fit in with the medium.

For a more complex design of this type, with solid blocks of color, it is preferable to print in a slightly different way. Cut out the block, but do not attach any form of holder to the back. Instead, ink the block and leave it (ink side up) on the work table.

Place a piece of the printing paper over the inked block and gently but firmly rub with a spoon handle, working from the center outward. (If the paper is fine and might tear, lay a second spare sheet of paper over the first before you start rubbing.) Do not pull the printed paper straight off the block: lift a corner carefully to see if more rubbing is needed. If it is, let the paper flop back into place again, and repeat the process.

Or you can put the lino block and paper into a screw-down press, sandwiching it between two sheets of cardboard, and press it for just a moment or two before removing it, ready to print another sheet.

Overprinting

If you become really proficient, you can even overprint in a second color. In this case, make all the prints you require in one color first, plus a few spares, then cut away further portions of the lino block and print over the first image a second time, using another color. The remaining parts of the block will print in the second color and the first color will show through in the areas which were cut away in between the two printings. Remember to allow ample time for the prints to dry between printing sessions. The important thing here is to align the paper absolutely accurately, so that the second printing does not blur over the first: this is a technique strictly for those with steady hands!

If you do not want to risk printing in a second color, you can bring in a second color by printing on colored paper.

Rather than printing directly onto cards, it is much simpler to make the prints and then glue these to cut and folded poster board or construction paper.

In addition to cards, you may also like to use one of your smaller Christmas motifs as a stamp to seal your Christmas card envelopes.

Christmas boxes

"It is more blessed to give than to receive" – and these little boxes are such fun to make that you may feel it is also more enjoyable. Taking care to wrap or package your gifts to look exciting and attractive is certainly an intrinsic part of the pleasure of giving. Whether you use these little boxes to enclose something expensive, like a bottle of perfume or a ring, or simply for a delicious treat such as a hand-made chocolate, they will enhance the pleasure for the recipient. Each of these boxes is simple to make, requiring only a few minutes' cutting and perhaps a dab of glue. The patterns can be enlarged to whatever size you choose, but it is generally best to keep them small and expensive-looking.

Cutting out

First, trace your chosen design. Cut carefully around the outline then use the resulting pattern to draw the outline on the poster board. Take care to make the poster board outline as accurate as possible, and make the pencil marks on the wrong side of the poster board.

Using the X-acto knife, carefully cut around the outline. Make sure that you rest the poster board on a proper cutting surface, such as a piece of fiberboard: it's hard to cut accurately if you are worrying about the table at the same time. Lean the blade against the edge of the metal ruler when cutting along straight lines and cut away from the hand that is holding the ruler, as far as this is possible.

Before you start assembling the box, score along the foldlines with a blunt, pointed tool such as the end of a knitting needle and then fold along these lines.

Read through the directions before you start assembling the box. If you are in any doubt as to how it works, experiment with the paper pattern or, if you intend to use this again, make a

tracing of the diagram as given in the book and assemble this smaller version as a trial piece.

House box

Cut out the shape and fold along the dotted foldlines. If you intend to use this box for anything weighty, or if you are making a larger version, it would be advisable to add a little glue to tabs 1 to 4, to give the box added strength. If this is not the case, then the finished box should hold together without glue.

Hold the two chimney tabs together and slip them through slot A. Finally, close the box by sliding tab 5 into slot B.

Apply small decorative details such as stickers: yellow windows and a blue door, for example, were used on the box shown here. Or you could paint or draw in details. If you are using the box to give a small present to a friend you might like to color and number the door the same as his or her real front door.

Holly box

This box is even simpler to make than the house box. The basic construction of interlocking pieces is one that is frequently used in box design because of its strength and also, perhaps, because the top is correspondingly more elaborate and decorative than a conventional box lid. If you look at any selection of perfume boxes you will almost certainly find several examples of this type of design.

Cut out the flat shape and fold along the dotted lines A, B, C and D. Cut around the solid outline of the holly leaves, but make sure that you leave them attached to the box by the dotted foldlines.

Glue tab 1 in position, to hold the sides of the box in place. At the base of the box, fold line E inwards, then fold line F, bringing tab 2 in so that the pointed end slips under slot A. Fold along line G, doing the same with tab 3.

Secure the base of the box by

Materials

Poster board

Scraps of colored paper; star stickers; round and rectangular stickers in various colors; paints or felt-tipped pens (optional – the choice of decorating materials is very varied and you can use whatever you already have in stock)

Pencil and metal ruler

X-acto knife

Clear glue

The amount of paper and poster board needed for the individual boxes is as follows:

House box – 11¾in x 8in
Holly box – 9in x 4¾in
Bird box – 9in x 6¼in
Christmas tree box – 11¾in x 7⅜in
Star box – 11in x 7⅜in

folding along line H and slipping tab 4 into slot A, taking it over the tops of tabs 2 and 3.

To finish the box, fold tabs 5 and 6 inward along lines I and J, then fold along line K. Fold along line L bringing the two holly leaves through slot B. When you have pulled the holly leaves through the slot, fold them down again to close the box. From green paper cut two holly leaves for the top decoration and stick on gold stars around the box sides and lid. Or, instead, the holly leaves could be painted green, or you could cover them with green foil, for a sparkling finishing touch.

Bird box

This box is an adaptation of the holly box, the main difference being that in this case the box is held shut by a small bird.

Cut out the box shape and fold along lines A, B, C and D. Glue tab 1 into position to hold the sides together. At the base of the box, fold along line E, bringing slot A inward. Fold along F and G and slip the pointed ends of tabs 2 and 3 under slot A. Finally slip tab 4 under slot A, above tabs 2 and 3.

Trace over the bird shape. Cut out and use it as a pattern to mark the outline on poster board. Using an X-acto knife, carefully cut out the bird from poster board. Score along the dotted foldlines at the back of the card with a knitting needle, pressing slightly, to make the poster board easier to fold accurately.

The bird shape is very easy to make once you are used to the way in which it works, but you may find it helpful to fold a paper copy first, so that you do not risk spoiling the poster board. First fold the piece in half lengthwise, with wrong sides together. (You will see the bird taking shape more easily if you hold the shape with the wings pointing upward.)

Gently push the tail upward between the wings along the V-shaped fold line marked A. Bring the other, front end of the bird up between the wings, folding along line B. Push the head portion down into the neck, folding along the V-shaped line C. When the wings are opened out the neck, head and tail should now unfold into a bird shape.

Return to the box and glue the bird in position along the dotted lines marked on tab 7. Put the box to one side until you are sure that the glue has dried and the bird is firmly secured to the tab, then lift tab 7 and fold tabs 5 and 6 in along lines I and J. Fold tab 7 over them, then fold along line L and, keeping the wings of the bird closed, bring slot B down so that the bird passes through it. Open out the wings of the bird to keep the box closed. Stick on gold stars.

This box, like the others, can be decorated in various ways. You could, for example, paint in details of the head and feathers on the bird, using a fine sable paintbrush, or you could spray the bird with gold or silver, masking off the rest of the box.

Christmas tree box

This box requires more folding than the previous styles. Cut out the shape, as already described, and score along the foldlines on the back of the poster board with a knitting needle or similar blunt, pointed tool. Fold along the dotted lines, taking each fold in turn and then opening the piece out: this will make the construction easier.

Fold along lines A, B, C and D and glue tabs 1 and 2 in place. At the base of the box fold tabs 3, 4, 5 and 6 inward, in that order, so that the rounded part of each tab lies under the previous tab. The rounded part of tab 3 slips under tab 6, securing the base.

The tabs which form the top of the box are all joined at the sides, but it is easier to complete the top if you consider them as separate. First, fold out the pointed tree sections so that each one faces outward from the box

Trace pattern for house box

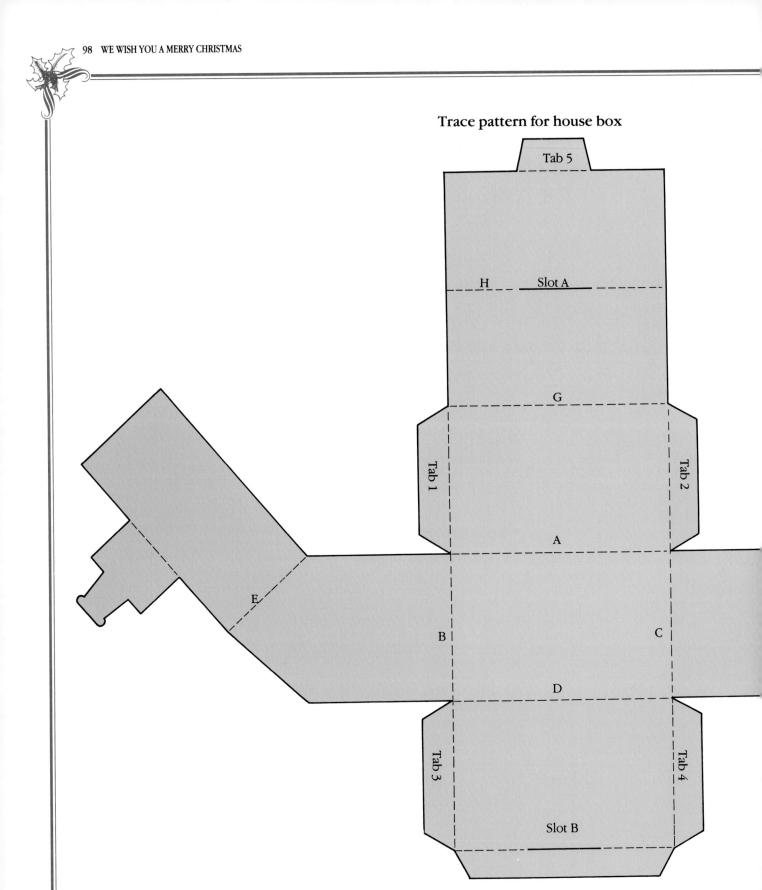

Trace pattern for bird

C   C

B   B

A   A

*To make the bird box, omit
the holly leaves and glue the
bird on dotted outline* M.

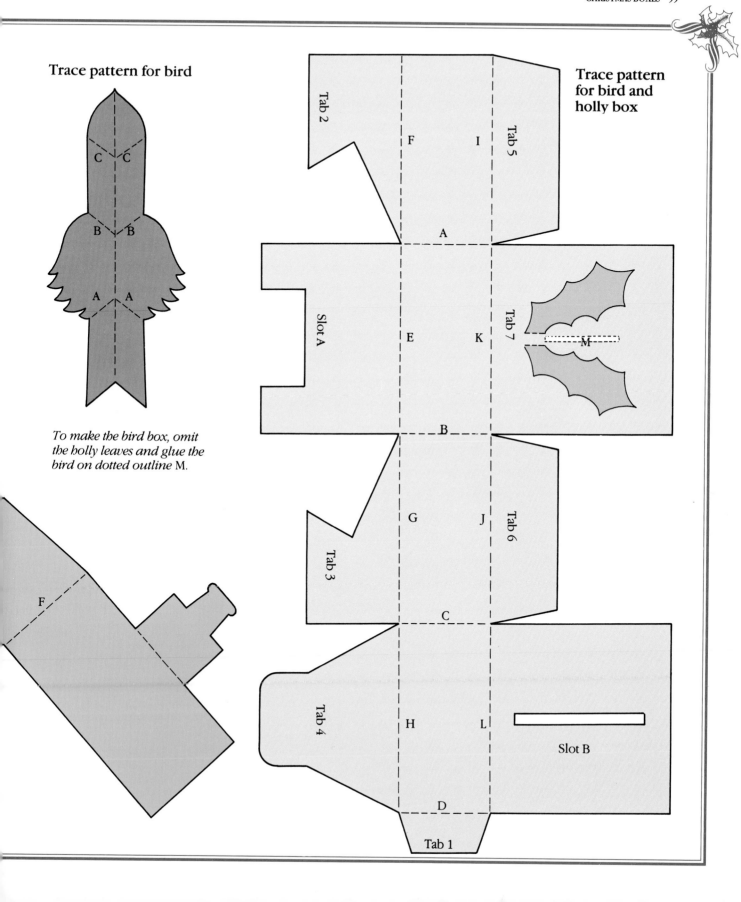

Tab 2

F   I

Tab 5

A

Slot A

E   K

Tab 7

M

B

G   J

Tab 6

Tab 3

C

F

Tab 4

H   L

Slot B

D

Tab 1

Trace pattern for Christmas tree box

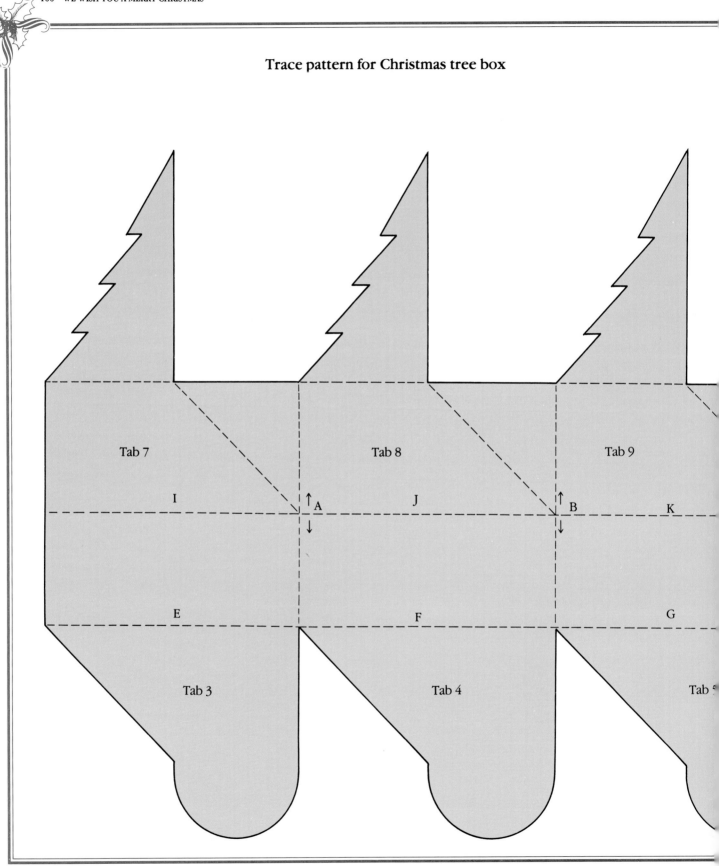

and at right angles to the tab to which it is joined.

Taking tabs 7, 8, 9 and 10 one at a time, as far as this is possible, fold each tab inward in sequence. Fold along the diagonal, bringing half of line A toward line I, half of line B towards line J and so on. As each tab is folded in, the next will start to follow it. Eventually, when the box is half closed, all the tabs will be pulling each other toward the center, and each will overlap the next. When all the tabs are folded down, stand the tree sections in a pyramid tree shape so that they support each other.

Decorate the box appropriately, covering the tree sections with colored "ornaments" (round stickers) or small gold stars.

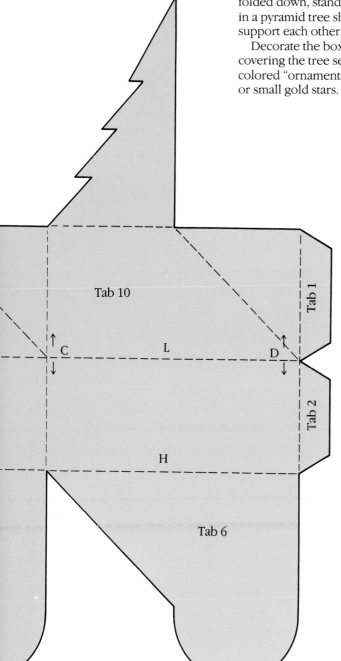

Trace pattern for star box

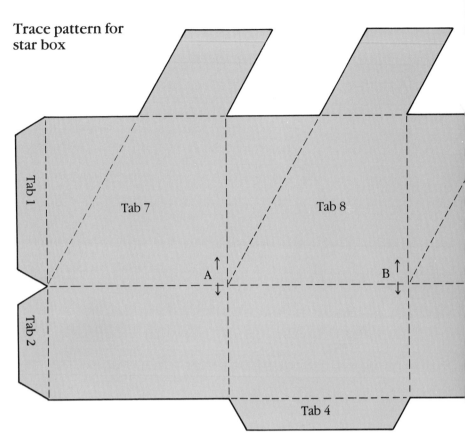

Star box

Cut out the shape as described and fold along each dotted line before you start constructing the box.

To put the box together, start by folding along lines A, B, C and D and gluing tabs 1 and 2 in position. Next fold up the pentagonal base and glue tabs 3, 4, 5 and 6 in position.

When the glue has dried and the tabs are securely in position, start folding in the top of the box. Although the tabs at the top are all joined at the side it is best to think of them as being separate. Begin to ease them into the center of the box one at a time. As each tab is folded, it will draw in its neighbor: make sure that each tab is folded to lie under the next one along – 7 under 8, 8 under 9 and so on. Tab 11 will fold under tab 7 on the fully closed box.

To keep the box as neat as possible,

begin very gently until you see what is happening. If necessary, make a paper model first. Finally, fold out the diamond shapes on each tab to form a five-pointed star, and cover with gold paper. Decorate the box with gold stars randomly stuck on.

Hanging the box

In olden days, people loved to festoon their Christmas trees with tiny boxes like these, each one containing a sugar plum or a chocolate, or perhaps a small trinket for a friend who would be visiting over the festive season. All of these boxes can readily be adapted for this purpose, provided the contents are not awkward shapes or too heavy.

A thread could be run through the chimney stack of the house, for instance. You could make a small hole at the center of tab 7 of the holly box

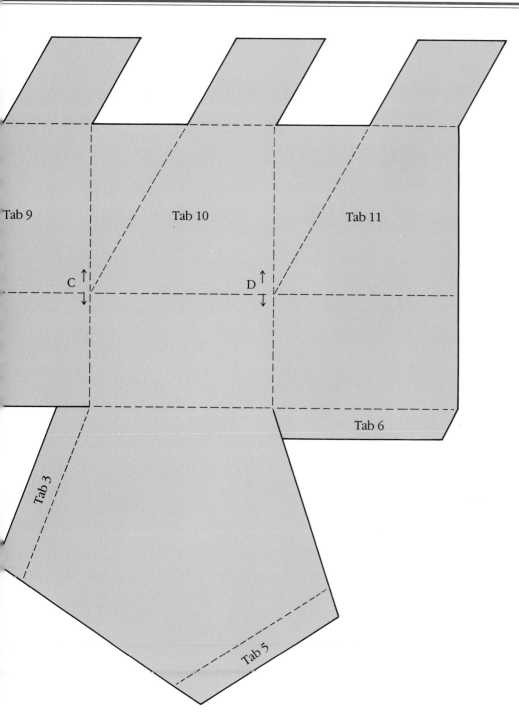

Tab 9

Tab 10

Tab 11

C

D

Tab 6

Tab 3

Tab 5

and draw a thread through, knotting the end to hold the box. For the bird box you could run gold threads through the four corners, knotting each underneath the tab and tying them together above the bird, making a little cage. You could secure the top of the tree to a hanging thread with gold star stickers, and fold the star box over a knotted ribbon.

CHAPTER 4

'Twas the night before Christmas

For children, the real fun of Christmas Day begins early in the morning with the eagerly anticipated discovery that their stockings have been mysteriously filled. Children love to make their own family traditions for Christmas and any of the handmade stockings – crocheted, knitted or appliquéd – shown on these and the following pages, could quickly become part of the tradition of your family. Regretfully packed away when Christmas is over, they will be ceremoniously brought out of hiding and hung up to greet Santa year after year, and there are plenty of designs so that each child can have his or her individual stocking.

Materials

Knitting worsted weight yarn in amounts and colors as foll:

Christmas tree stocking

6oz in red

1oz in green

Small amounts of pink, blue, light green, red, yellow and tan

Cotton

Candle stocking

5oz in white

2oz each in blue and green

1oz in red

Small amount of yellow

Batting

Santa Claus stocking

6oz in red

4oz in white

1oz in pink

Small amount of blue

Cotton

Ice skating stocking

6oz in black

2oz in yellow

1oz in white

Cardboard

Size F crochet hook (all stockings)

Tapestry needle

Gauge

15 hdc and 12 rows to 4in on size F hook.

See crochet abbreviations, page 109

Crocheted stockings

Here are four delightful designs, all crocheted to the same basic pattern to make a firm stocking that can be filled to the brim with surprise Christmas presents. Each stocking measures 24½in long and has a circumference at the top of 18in.

Basic stocking

Using size F hook, ch 35.

Base row 1 hdc in 3rd ch from hook, 1hdc in each ch to end. Turn. 34 hdc.

1st-5th rows Ch 2 to count as first hdc, 1 hdc in each st to end. Turn.

6th row Ch 2, work 2 hdc tog, work to last 3 sts, work 2 hdc tog, 1 hdc in last st. Turn. 32 hdc.

Rep last 6 rows 5 times more. 22 hdc. Work 5 rows even.

42nd row Ch 2, 2 hdc in next st, work to last 2 sts, 2 hdc in next st, 1 hdc in last st. Turn. 24 hdc.

43rd row As first row.

Rep last 2 rows twice more, then first of them again. 30 hdc.

49th row As first row.

50th row Ch 2, work to last 2 sts, 2 hdc in next st, 1 hdc in last st. Turn.

51st row Ch 2, 2 hdc, in next st, work to last 3 sts, work 2 hdc tog, 1 hdc in last st. Turn.

52nd row Ch 2, work 2 hdc tog, work to last 2 sts, 2 hdc in last st. Turn.

53rd row Ch 2, work 2 hdc in next st, work to last 5 sts, (work 2 hdc tog) twice, 1 hdc in last st. Turn.

54th row Ch 2, (work 2 hdc tog) twice, work to last 2 sts, 2 hdc in next st, 1 hdc in last st. Turn.

Rep last 2 rows once.

57th row Ch 2, 2 hdc in next st, work to last 3 sts, work 2 hdc tog, 1 hdc in last st. Turn.

58th row Ch 2, work 2 hdc tog, work to last 2 sts, 2 hdc in next st, 1 hdc in last st. Turn.

Rep last 2 rows twice more.

63rd row Ch 2, work 2 hdc tog, work to last 5 sts, (work 2 hdc tog) twice, 1 hdc in last st. Turn.

64th row Ch 2, (work 2 hdc tog) twice, work to last 3 sts, work 2 hdc tog, 1 hdc in last st. Turn.

Rep last 2 rows twice more. Fasten off. Make a 2nd piece in the same way.

Christmas tree stocking

Using red yarn, make 2 pieces as given for basic stocking.

Finishing

Hold the 2 pieces of stocking tog, matching shape. Using size F hook, red yarn and with RS of work facing, beg at top and join shapes by working a row of sc evenly through edge st of both thicknesses.

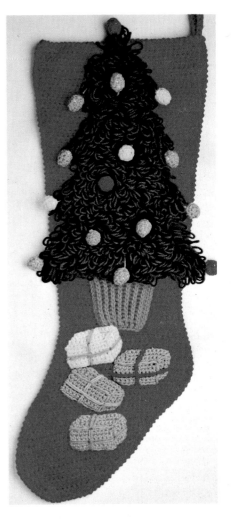

Do not turn, but work a row of crab st (sc worked from left to right) around shape, then cont around top. Fasten off.

Loop
Using size F hook and red, ch 31. Working over a length of string, work 1 sc in 2nd ch from hook, 1 sc in each ch to end, turn. Working over string, work another row in sc. Fasten off.

Fold into a loop and sew to top of stocking to hang it up.**

Tree
Using size F hook and green yarn, ch 39.
Base row 1 sc in 2nd ch from hook, 1 sc in each ch to end. Turn. 38 sc.
1st row (RS) Ch 1, 1 sc in first sc, wrap yarn over and under index finger of left hand, insert hook in next sc, yo

Trace pattern for skate blade

and draw a loop through, yo and complete sc in usual way – called 1 loop st – 1 loop st in each sc to last sc, 1 sc in last sc. Turn.

2nd row Ch 1, 1 sc in first st, work 2 sc tog, work in sc to last 3 sts, work 2 sc tog, 1 sc in last st. Turn.

Rep first and 2nd rows 7 times more. 22 sts.

17th row Ch 6, sl st in 2nd ch from hook, 1 loop st in each of next 4 ch, work in loop st to end. Turn.

18th row Ch 6, 1 sc in 2nd ch from hook, 2 sc tog over next 2 ch, 1 sc into each of next 2 ch, work in sc to last 3 sts, 2 sc tog, 1 sc in last st. Turn. 30 sts.

19th row As first (loop) row.

20th row Ch 1, 1 sc in first st, 2 sc tog, work in sc to last 3 sts, 2 sc tog, 1 sc in last st. Turn.

Rep last 2 rows 6 times more. 16 sts.

33rd and 34th rows Inc as given for 17th and 18th rows. 24 sts.

Rep 19th and 20th rows 6 times more. 12 sts.

47th and 48th rows Inc as given for 17th and 18th rows. 20 sts.

Rep 19th and 20th rows until 6 sts rem.

Next row Ch 1, 1 sc in each of first 2 sts, 2 sc tog, 1 sc in each of next 2 sts. Turn.

Next row As first row.

Next row Ch 1, 1 sc, in first st, 2 sc tog twice. Turn.

Next row As first row.

Next row Ch 1, 2 sc tog, 1 sc in last st. Turn.

Next row Ch 1, 1 loop st in first st wrapping yarn 3 times around finger 1 sc into last st. Fasten off.

Tub

Using size F hook and tan yarn, ch 16. Beg crochet rib pat as foll:

Base row 1 hdc in 3rd ch from hook, 1 hdc in each ch to end. Turn. 15 hdc.

1st row Ch 2, skip first hdc, *yo and insert from front to back and to front again around post of next hdc, complete hdc in usual way, rep from * to end, 1 hdc in turning ch. Turn.

Rep first row 12 times more.

14th row (RS) Ch 1, 1 sc in each st to end. Fasten off.

Work in sc along one side edge to form lower edge of tub.

Ornaments

Using size F hook and any color, ch 3 and join with a sl st to first ch to form a ring.

1st round Ch 1, 4 sc in ring, join with a sl st to first ch.

2nd round Ch 1, 2 sc in each sc to end, with a sc in first ch. 8 sc.

3rd round Ch 1, 1 sc in each sc to end, join with a sl st to first ch.

4th round Ch 1, (2 sc tog) 4 times, join with a sl st to first ch. Fasten off, leaving a long end for stitching. Pad with cotton. Draw sts tog to close top, leaving a long end to sew to tree.

Make 3 ornaments in each color.

Presents

Using size F hook and any color, ch 11.

Base row 1 sc in 2nd ch from hook, 1 sc in each ch to end. Turn. 10 sc.

1st row Ch 1, 1 sc in each st to end. 10 sc.

Rep last row 3 times more.

Working down one side edge, ch 1, 2 sc tog, 1 sc in each row end to corner st, 3 sc in corner, 1 sc in each st to last 2 sts, 2 sc tog. Turn.

Work 3 more rows in this way, dec one st at each end and inc 3 sts at corner. Fasten off, leaving a long end. Thread end into a tapestry needle and embroider a line of stem stitch as shown in the photograph. Use a length of a contrasting color to embroider ties.

Make 3 more presents in different colors. Sew tub to base of tree and ornaments to tree. Assemble tree and presents as shown and stitch to one side of sock only.

Ice skating stocking

Using black yarn, work as given for Christmas tree stocking to **, omitting crab st edging.

Skate

Using size F hook and white yarn, ch 5.

Base row 1 sc in 2nd ch from hook, 1 sc to each ch to end. Turn. 4 sc.
Work 8 rows in sc.
9th row Ch 3, 1 sc into 3rd ch from hook, 1 sc in each st to end. Turn. 6 sc.
10th-13th rows Work in sc.
14th row Ch 1, 1 sc in each of next 4 sc. Turn.
15th-32nd rows Work in sc.
33rd row As 9th row.
34th-37th rows Work in sc.
38th row As 14th row.
39th-68th rows Work in sc.
69th row Ch 1, 1 sc in each of next 2 sc, 2 sc tog. Turn.
70th row Work in sc.
71st row Ch 1, 1 sc in next sc, 2 sc tog. Turn.
72nd row Ch 1, 2 sc tog.
Fasten off. Make a 2nd piece in the same way. Cut a skate in cardboard and sew 2 crochet pieces of skate tog with cardboard in between.

Trim

Using size F hook and yellow yarn, ch 5.

Base row 1 sc in 2nd ch from hook, 1 sc in each ch to end. Turn. 4 sc.
1st row Ch 1, 2 sc in first st, 1 sc in each st to end. Turn. 5 sc.
2nd row Ch 1, 1 sc in each st to last st, 2 sc in last st. Turn. 6 sc.
Rep last 2 rows 3 times more. 12 sc.
9th row Ch 1, 1 sc in each st to end. Turn.
10th row Ch 1, 1 sc in each st to last 3 sts, 2 sc tog, 1 sc in last st. Turn.
11th row Ch 1, 1 sc in next st, 2 sc tog, 1 sc in each st to end. Turn.
Rep last 2 rows 3 times more. 4 sc.
18th row As 9th row.
Rep these 18 rows 4 times more.
Next row Ch 1, 1 sc in next sc, 2 sc tog, 1 sc in last st. Turn.
Next row As 9th row.
Next row Ch 1, 1 sc in first sc, 2 sc tog. Turn.
Next row Ch 1, 2 sc tog. Fasten off.

Make a 2nd piece in the same way. Join 2 pieces tog at straight edge. Using black yarn, work in crab st around pointed edge of trim. Using black yarn, make a chain 81in long for lace. Thread lace through trim, finishing at top with a bow. Sew trim to boot, matching center seams. Sew skate to lower edge of boot. Using size F hook, yellow yarn and with RS of work facing, work in sc around top of boot, do not turn, but work a row of crab st. Fasten off.

Santa Claus stocking

Work as given for Christmas tree stocking to **

Face

Using size F hook and pink yarn, ch 11.
Base row 1 sc in 2nd ch from hook, 1 sc in each ch to end. Turn. 10 sc.
1st row Ch 1, 2 sc in first sc, 1 sc in each sc to last sc, 2 sc in last sc. Turn. 2 sc increased.
Rep last rows 8 times more. 28 sc.
10th-20th rows Ch 1, 1 sc in each sc to end. Turn.
21st row As first row. 30 sc.
22nd-27th rows Work in sc.
28th row As firsr row. 32 sc.
29th-33rd rows Work in sc.
34th row As first row. 34 sc.
35th-38th rows Work in sc.
39th row Ch 1, 2 sc tog, 1 sc in each sc to last 2 sc, 2 sc tog. Turn. 2 sts decreased.
40th row Ch 1, 1 sc in each sc to end. Turn. Rep last 2 rows 3 times more. 26 sts. Fasten off.

Beard

Using size F hook and white yarn, ch 17.
Base row 1 sc in 2nd ch from hook, 1 sc into each ch to end. Turn. 16 sc.
1st row Ch 1, 1 sc in first sc, 1 loop st (see Christmas tree directions) in each st to last st, 1 sc in last st. Turn.
2nd row Ch 1, 1 sc in each st to end. Turn.
3rd row As first row.

Crochet abbreviations

beg	=	begin(ning)
ch	=	chain(s)
cont	=	continu(e)(ing)
dc	=	double crochet
dec	=	decreas(e)(ing)
dtr	=	double triple crochet
foll	=	follow(s)(ing)
gr(s)	=	group(s)
hdc	=	half double crochet
in	=	inch(es)
inc	=	increas(e)(ing)
oz	=	ounce(s)
pat	=	pattern
rem	=	remain(ing)
rep	=	repeat
RS	=	right side
sc	=	single crochet
sl st	=	slip stitch
sp	=	space(s)
st(s)	=	stitch(es)
tog	=	together
tr	=	treble crochet
tr tr	=	triple triple crochet
yo	=	yarn over hook

4th row Ch 1, 2 sc in first st, 1sc in each st to last st, 2 sc in last st. Turn. 2 sts increased.

Rep first-4th rows 7 times more, then work first row again. 32 sts.

34th row Ch 1, 1 sc in each of next 12 sc. Turn.

35th row As first row.

36th row Ch 1, 1 sc in each st to last 2 sts, 2 sc tog. Turn.

Rep 35th and 36th rows 9 times more. 2 sts.

55th row Ch 1, 1 loop st in each of next 2 sts. Turn.

56th row Ch 1, 2 sc tog. Turn.

57th row Ch 1, work a loop st in last st, but wrap yarn 3 times around finger.

Fasten off.

With RS of work facing, skip 8 sc, rejoin yarn to next st and work in sc to end. 12 sc.

Complete to match other side, reversing shaping.

Mustache

Using size F hook and white yarn, ch 7.

Base row 1 sc in 2nd ch from hook, 1 sc in each ch to end. Turn.

1st row Ch 3, 1 sc in 2nd ch from hook, 1 sc in next ch, 1 loop st in each st to last st, 1 sc in last st. Turn.

2nd row Sl st in each of first 2 sts, ch 1, 1 sc in each st to end. Turn.

Rep these 2 rows 3 times more.

9th row Ch 1, 1 sc in first st, 1 loop st in each st to last st, 1 sc in last st.

Fasten off.

Make a 2nd piece in the same way, reversing shaping.

Eyebrows

Using size F hook and white yarn, ch 13.

Base row 1 sc in 2nd ch from hook, 1 sc in each ch to end. Turn. 12 sc.

1st row As 9th row of mustache.

2nd row Ch 1, 1 sc in each st to end. Turn.

3rd row As first two.

Fasten off.

Make a 2nd piece in the same way.

Hat band

Using size F hook and white yarn, ch 31.

Base row 1 sc in 2nd ch from hook, 1 sc in each ch to end. Turn. 30 sc.

Work first and 2nd rows as for eyebrows 4 times.

Fasten off.

Cut all loops in half and unravel using a tapestry needle. Mold yarn of mustache and eyebrows to form a right and left side.

Nose

Using size F hook and red yarn, ch 3 and join with a sl st to first ch to form a ring.

Base round Ch 1, 4 sc in ring, join with a sl st to first sc.

1st round Ch 1, 2 sc in each sc to end, join with a sl st to first sc. 8 sc.

2nd round As first round. 16 sc.

3rd-4th rounds Ch 1, 1 sc in each sc to end, join with a sl st to first sc.

Fasten off, leaving a long end for stitching.

Pad nose with cotton, gather around edge and pull tog, but do not pull too tightly.

Eyes

Using size F hook and white yarn, ch 10. Skip 1 ch, 1 sc in next ch, 1 hdc in next ch, 1 dc in next ch, 1 tr in next ch, 1 dtr in next ch, 1 tr in next ch, 1 dc in next ch, 1 hdc in next ch, 1 sc in next ch.

Fasten off, leaving long end.

Make a 2nd piece in the same way.

Finishing

Sew beard to face, just overlapping at lower edge.

Sew nose 3½in above chin.

Stitch mustache under nose and eye about 2in above nose.

Using tapestry needle and red yarn, embroider mouth using satin stitch.

Using blue yarn, embroider eyes.

Sew on eyebrows.

Stitch face to one side of stocking.

Sew on hat band to cover join at top of face.

Candle stocking

Using white, make 2 pieces as given for basic stocking.

Finishing
Using red yarn, join tog and make loop as given for Christmas tree stocking to **.

Candle
Using size F hook and blue yarn, ch 23.
Base row 1 sc in 2nd ch from hook, 1 sc in each ch to end. Turn. 22 sc.
1st row Ch 1, 1 sc in each st to end. Turn.
Rep last row until work measures 13¾in from beg. Fasten off.
Circle for top
Using blue yarn, ch 3 and join with a sl st to first ch to form a ring.
Base round Ch 1, 4 sc in ring, join with a sl st to first sc.
1st round Ch 1, 2 sc in each sc, join with a sl st to first sc. 8 sc.
2nd round Ch 1, 1 sc in each sc to end, join with a sl st to first sc.
Rep last 2 rounds once more. Fasten off.

Flame
Using size F hook and red yarn, ch 4.
Base row 1 sc in 2nd ch from hook, 1 sc in each of next 2 ch. Turn. 3 sc.
1st row Ch 1, 1 sc in each sc to end. Turn.
2nd row Ch 1, 2 sc in first st, cont in sc to last st, 2 sc in last st. Turn. 2 sts increased.
Rep 2nd row 3 times more. 11 sc.
6th row As first row.
7th row Ch 1, 2 sc tog, 1 sc in each st to last 2 sts, 2 sc tog, joining in yellow on last st. Turn. Break off red.
8th row As first row.
9th row As 7th row, but using yellow only.
Rep last 2 rows twice more. 3 sc.
14th row Ch 1, 2 sc tog, 1 sc in last st. Turn.
15th row Ch 1, 2 sc tog.
Fasten off.

Make a 2nd piece in the same way. Join 2 long edges of candle tog and sew in circle using whipstitch to form top of candle.
Pad candle with batting until firm, then sew lower edges tog with seam to center back.
Sew 2 pieces of flame tog. Using yellow, work a few lines in straight stitch over the red. Sew flame to top of candle.

Holly leaves
Using size F hook and green yarn, ch 31.
Base row 1 sc in 2nd ch from hook, 1 sc in each ch to end. Turn. 30 sc.
1st row Ch 1, 1 sc in each of first 3 sts, 1 hdc in each of next 3 sts, 1 dc in each of next 2 sts, 2 tr in next st, 1 dtr in next st, 3 tr tr in next st, 1 dtr in next st, 2 tr in next st, 1 dc in each of next 5 sts, 2 tr in next st, 1 dtr in next st, 3 tr tr in next st, 1 dtr in next st, 2 tr in next st, 1 dc in each of next 2 sts, 1 hdc in each of next 2 sts, 1 sc in each of next 2 sts, 3 sc in last st to form point of leaf, then work other side of leaf as first, but reversing shaping. Turn.
Edging row Ch 1, 1 sc in each st to center of first tr tr group, work a picot (1 sc, ch 3, 1 sc in 3rd ch from hook), cont around leaf in this way, working a picot in center st of each point.
Make 4 more holly leaves in the same way.

Berries
Using size F hook and red yarn, ch 3 and join with a sl st to first ch to form a ring.
1st round Ch 1, 4 sc in ring, join with a sl st to first sc.
2nd round Ch 1, 1 sc in each sc, join with a sl st to first sc.
Fasten off, leaving a long end.
Pad with cotton and sew up.
Make 7 more berries in same way.
Sew candle to center of stocking as shown.
Arrange leaves at base of candle as shown and sew in position.
Sew on berries.

Scandinavian-style stockings

Lovely brightly-colored stockings with traditional Scandinavian motifs like the Norwegian star and Christmas symbols, including a snowman, a robin or a Santa Claus worked into the foot – any of them would make a lovely keepsake, ready to be reused next year. The pattern is graded for 5[7:8½] shoe sizes, so if you have the energy to knit two of each you will have seasonal, highly wearable presents. What could be nicer than on Christmas morning to find the companion sock rolled up in the toe of the present carrier?

Snowman A

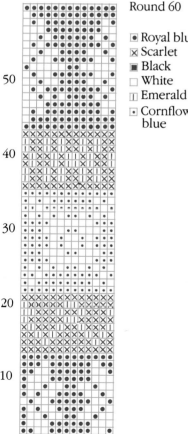

Round 60

- ● Royal blue
- ⊠ Scarlet
- ■ Black
- □ White
- ⏛ Emerald
- · Cornflower blue

Note

Strand colors not in use loosely across the WS of the work. Follow the instructions given below for the three stockings, but refer to the separate charts for each design. Yarn colors are shown in the order Snowman [Robin: Santa Claus].

The yarn quantity given for each stocking is enough for a matching pair.

To make

Using size 6 needles and scarlet [royal blue: yellow], cast on 52 sts, evenly spaced over 3 needles.
Work 18 rounds in K1, P1 ribbing. Cont working in rounds, beg working in st st from Chart A, reading each chart row from right to left and noting that 1 pat rep is worked 4 times in all. Cont in cornflower blue [emerald: royal blue] and work 1 round, dec 1 st at end of round. 51 sts.

Shape heel

Next round K13 sts, turn, P24 sts, turn. Using 2 needles, work 20 rows more in st st on these 24 sts.

Snowman B

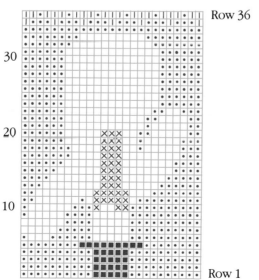

Row 36

Row 1

Materials

Knitting worsted weight yarn in amounts and colors as foll:

Snowman stocking
1¾oz each in royal blue, white, scarlet, black, cornflower blue and emerald green

Robin stocking
1¾oz each in yellow, brown, white, scarlet, royal blue, bottle green and emerald green

Santa Claus stocking
1¾oz each in yellow, scarlet, white, royal blue and brown
Set of four size 6 double-pointed needles (all stockings)

Gauge

22 sts and 30 rows to 4in on size 6 needles over st st.

Knitting abbreviations

approx	=	approximately
beg	=	beginning
cont	=	continue
dec	=	decrease(e)(ing)
foll	=	follow(s)(ing)
in	=	inch(es)
inc	=	increase(e)(ing)
K	=	knit
M1	=	make a stitch by picking up the strand between stitch just worked and next stitch and working into back of it
oz	=	ounce(s)
pat(s)	=	pattern(s)
P	=	purl
psso	=	pass slipped stitch over
rem	=	remain(s)(ing)
rep	=	repeat(ing)
RS	=	right side
sl	=	slip
st(s)	=	stitch(es)
st st	=	stockinette stitch
tbl	=	through back of loop
tog	=	together
WS	=	wrong side

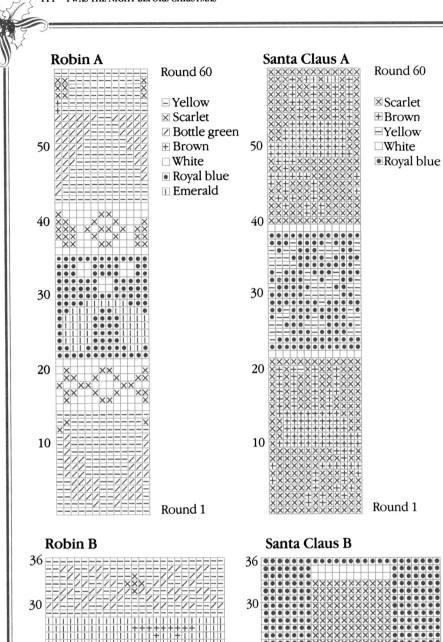

Robin A

Round 60

□ Yellow
☒ Scarlet
☑ Bottle green
⊞ Brown
□ White
⊡ Royal blue
⊟ Emerald

Round 1

Santa Claus A

Round 60

☒ Scarlet
⊞ Brown
⊟ Yellow
□ White
⊡ Royal blue

Round 1

Robin B

Row 1

Santa Claus B

Row 1

Next row Turn, K16 sts, sl 1, K1, psso.
***Next row** Turn, sl 1 purlwise, P8, P 2 tog.
Next row Turn, sl 1 knitwise, K8, sl 1, K1, psso.*
Rep from * to * until 10 sts rem.
Cont with four needles.
Next row K10, pick up and K11 sts from side of heel, K 27 sts, pick up and K11 sts from side of heel. 59 sts.
Next row K22, K first row from Chart B over next 25 sts, inc 1, turn.
Next row P1, P 2nd row of Chart B, P rem 34 sts, inc 1, turn. 61 sts.
Next row K1, sl 1, K1, psso, K30, K 2 tog, K 3rd row of Chart B, K1, turn. 59 sts.
Next row P1, P 4th row of Chart B, P33, turn.
Next row K1, sl 1, K1, psso, K28, K 2 tog, K 5th row of Chart B, K1, turn. 57 sts.
Next row P1, P 6th row of Chart B, P31, turn.
Cont working in rows in pat from Chart B, working heel shaping as above until 51 sts rem. Work even until all 36 rows of Chart B have been completed.
Next row Change to emerald [royal blue: yellow], sl 1, K1, psso, K to last 2 sts, K2 tog. 49 sts.
Cont working in rounds on all sts until foot measures 7[7½:8] in.
Divide sts between 3 needles as foll:
First and 2nd needles – 12 sts;
3rd needle – 25 sts.
Shape toe
Next round First needle – Sl 1, K1, psso, K to end; 2nd needle – K to last 2 sts, K2 tog; 3rd needle – sl 1, K1, psso, K to last 2 sts, K2 tog.
Rep last round until 17 sts rem. Break off yarn, leaving 15¾in length of yarn. Graft ends of toe tog. Fasten off.

Finishing

Weave in ends and join foot seams. Turn each sock to WS, fit over a rolled-up towel, and press lightly following pressing instructions on yarn label. Embroider features on Snowman in black and scarlet yarn.

Reindeer stocking

Rudolph the red-nosed reindeer (with a little bird to keep him company) waits by the chimney while Santa Claus fills the stockings. This tiny needlepoint stocking should last for years, and in fact there is no reason why, with care, it should not become a family heirloom to be passed down within the family as a minor Christmas tradition. Its small scale – it measures approximately 8½in from the top to the base of the foot and 7in across at the foot – along with the care that goes into its making seem to demand that it should be filled with extra-special gifts.

The quantities given assume that the stocking is backed with the same material as the lining, but you could if you wish back it with a firm velvet for added luxury. Whatever fabric you choose, make sure that it is firm enough and will not stretch.

Working the design

First trace over the main outline of the stocking (the finer details can simply be copied from the chart) and transfer it to the canvas, as described on page 84, leaving a margin of at least 2in all around. Do not trim the canvas at this stage.

To prevent the work from becoming distorted, it is preferable to put the canvas in a needlepoint frame – this also means that you have both hands free for working.

If you do not have a frame you could simply thumbtack the edges of the canvas to an old picture frame.

If you intend to work without a frame, bind the edges of the canvas with masking tape to prevent them from raveling and catching the yarn as you work.

Starting from the center and working outward, embroider the entire design in either continental stitch (see page 84) or half cross stitch, which looks the same as continental stitch from the right side but uses only half the amount of yarn. If you are using half cross stitch you should also check carefully to make sure that you are covering the canvas threads completely.

To work half cross stitch (see opposite) bring your needle out at the top left-hand side of the area to be worked. Insert the needle diagonally upward over a single intersection and bring it out one horizontal thread below. Work along the row, making small, slanting stitches; the stitches on the reverse side will run vertically.

If you are using continental stitch, work in diagonal lines of stitches as much as possible, as the horizontal and vertical stitches on the back of the work will help to prevent the canvas from becoming distorted. Remember also to work with an even tension and do not pull the stitching too tightly.

By the time you have finished stitching, the work may have been pulled a little out of shape however hard you have tried to avoid this. In this case, you must block it to pull it back into shape and give it a smooth, well-finished appearance. If the work is very distorted, you may need to repeat the blocking process several times.

To block needlepoint, first dampen the back of the work with a damp cloth or a laundry spray to soften the stiffening agent in the canvas, then pull it gently into shape as much as possible. Draw the correct dimensions of the canvas on a piece of paper and tape the paper to a board. Place the canvas face down over the paper and thumbtack the edges to the board, using the paper markings as a guide and stretching the canvas evenly. Leave it to dry naturally for 24 hours or more, before removing it from the board.

Making the stocking

Cut away the spare canvas around the stocking, leaving ⅝in unworked for a seam allowance.

Using the canvas outline as a pattern

Materials

12in x 10in piece of 10-mesh-to-the-inch mono canvas
   (lockweave is the best choice to avoid raveling, or you could use double-mesh canvas if you prefer)
⅜yd of 36in-wide red satin for backing and binding
Anchor tapestry wool as follows:
   one skein each of white #0402, red #0334, green #0257, gold #0735 (only one yard needed), and browns #0418 and #0380 (only two yards of #0380 needed); two skeins of blue #0146, plus a small length of black for the eyes
Red sewing thread
Size #18 tapestry needle

Half cross stitch

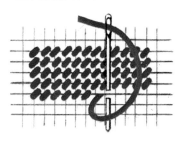

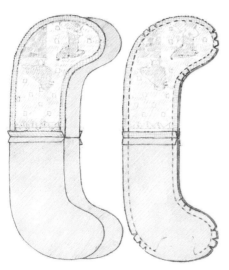

and following the cutting layout, cut three pieces from the red satin: one piece to form backing for all the needlepoint stocking and two pieces for the lining.

Place one lining section and the needlepoint stocking right sides together and stitch straight across the top of the stocking with a ⅝in seam. Trim and press the seam open. Repeat with the remaining fabric pair.

With the seams matching, place two sections right sides together. Pin, baste and then stitch around the edges, leaving a 4in gap at the base of the needlepoint stocking for turning right side out. Before turning the stocking to the right side, trim the seam

allowance and clip into the seam allowance on the inward curve. Cut notches from the seam allowance of the outward curves to reduce bulk.

Turn the stocking right side out and slip stitch the opening at the foot.

Insert the lining into the stocking and finger-press the top edge.

From spare satin, cut a piece measuring 6¼in x 1¼in. Fold this down the center, right sides together, and stitch along the length, making a ¼in seam. Turn the tube right side out and fold the raw ends inside the tube. Bring the ends together to make a loop and stitch the loop firmly in place to the inside back of the stocking.

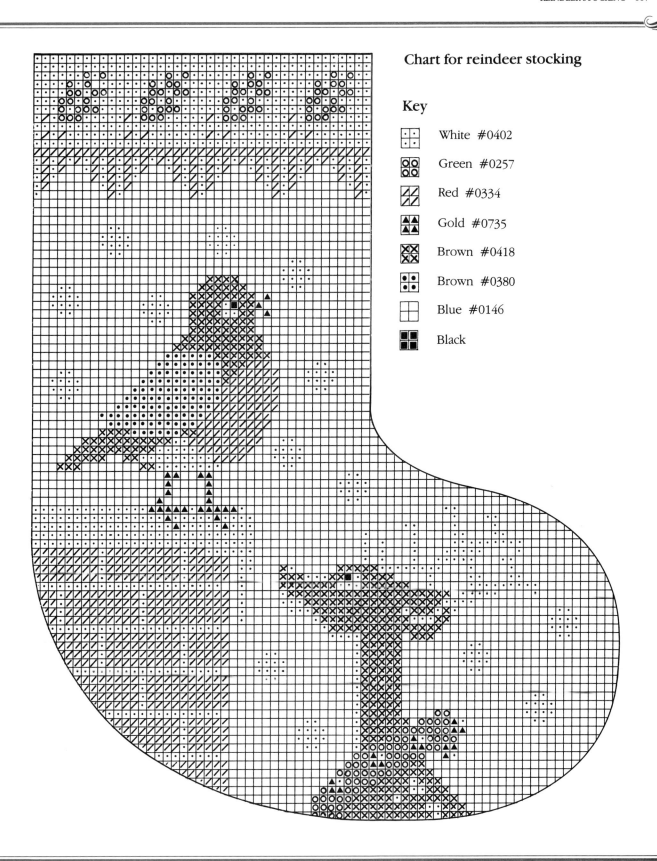

Chart for reindeer stocking

Key

White #0402	
Green #0257	
Red #0334	
Gold #0735	
Brown #0418	
Brown #0380	
Blue #0146	
Black	

Materials

5/8yd of 36in-wide green cotton fabric
5/8yd of 36in-wide white cotton fabric
5/8yd of lightweight polyester batting
1yd of 1in red bias binding
1yd of thin corded piping
1yd of gold tubular cording
1/4yd of 3/4in-wide gold ribbon
Green, white, red and gold sewing
  thread
Dressmaker's carbon paper
Tracing paper

Greetings stocking

This stylish Christmas stocking is decorated in French style, with Noël embroidered on the side in couched gold cording. Padded and lined in white with a turn-down top edged with red piping, the stocking measures approximately 4in across and 11¼in in length. Fill it with nuts and candy to make a traditional Christmas extra for a child, or tuck in small, more expensive gifts for an adult.

Although the end result is so chic, the stocking is relatively easy to make, so perhaps you could make a set, with one for each member of the family, each one decorated with Christmas written in a different language.

Preparing the pieces

First enlarge the stocking design onto graph paper then make a tracing paper pattern, and include the lettering as well as matching the registration marks.

Using the pattern as a template, draw around it to make three matching pairs of stockings: one pair on the green fabric, one on the white fabric and one on the batting, but do not cut out at this stage.

Take dressmaker's carbon paper and transfer the lettering to the right side of one green stocking piece: lay the fabric on a flat surface and tape it down at the corners with masking tape to hold it firm. Tape the pattern over the fabric, matching the outlines, then slip the carbon paper, carbon side down, between the pattern and the fabric. Trace over the lettering with a pencil, transferring the outline to the fabric.

Remove the dressmaker's carbon paper, pattern and tape from the fabric. Using matching gold thread and catching the gold cording from the underside only, carefully sew the cording in place, securing the ends firmly in position with several neat couching stitches placed close together. Or, instead, you could sew the entire design in satin stitch except for the two dots above the "o." These are worked as two French knots in gold thread.

To make the piping, fold and baste the red bias binding evenly over the corded piping. Using the zipper foot on the sewing machine, stitch close to the cording, enclosing it completely, keeping the edges even.

Cut out all three pairs of stockings from the fabrics.

Finishing

With right sides matching, stitch the green pair together with a ⅜in seam, leaving it open across the top and partway down both the back and front seams, as shown.

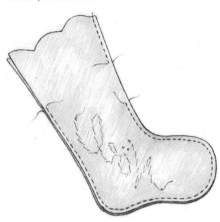

Take one white piece and a corresponding section of batting and stitch them together (placing the batting against the wrong side of the fabric) with a scant ⅜in seam. Stitch the batting to the second white piece in exactly the same way.

With the batting on the outside and making a ⅜in seam, stitch the two padded sections together, again leaving the top edge and the top of the back seam unsewn.

Turn the white stocking right side out and then pin and baste the prepared piping in position all around the top edge and the opening down

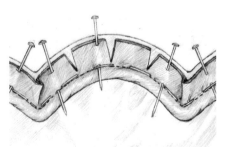

the back seam. The raw edges of the piping should match the raw edges of the stocking. Using white thread and the zipper foot of the sewing machine, stitch the piping to the stocking top, making sure that the ends of the cording are joined neatly together at the base of the back opening.

Trim away the seam allowances of the batting, cutting as close to the stitching as possible, in order to reduce the bulk.

Turn the green stocking wrong side out and put the white one inside it, so that the right side of the white stocking matches the right side of the green one. Using white thread and the zipper foot, stitch all around the piped opening, sewing as close as possible to the cording to cover all previous stitching.

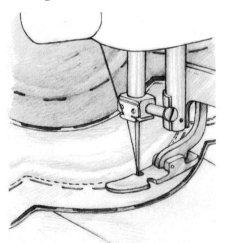

Bring the white stocking out through the opening on the front seam of the green stocking, then turn the green stocking right side out through the same opening. Fold the white stocking down inside the green one.

Close the opening, using matching green thread and neat slip stitches. Fold the stocking down at the top to show the white, piped edging.

Take the gold ribbon and fold it in half. Sew it neatly to the inside of the stocking at the top of the back seam to make a hanging loop.

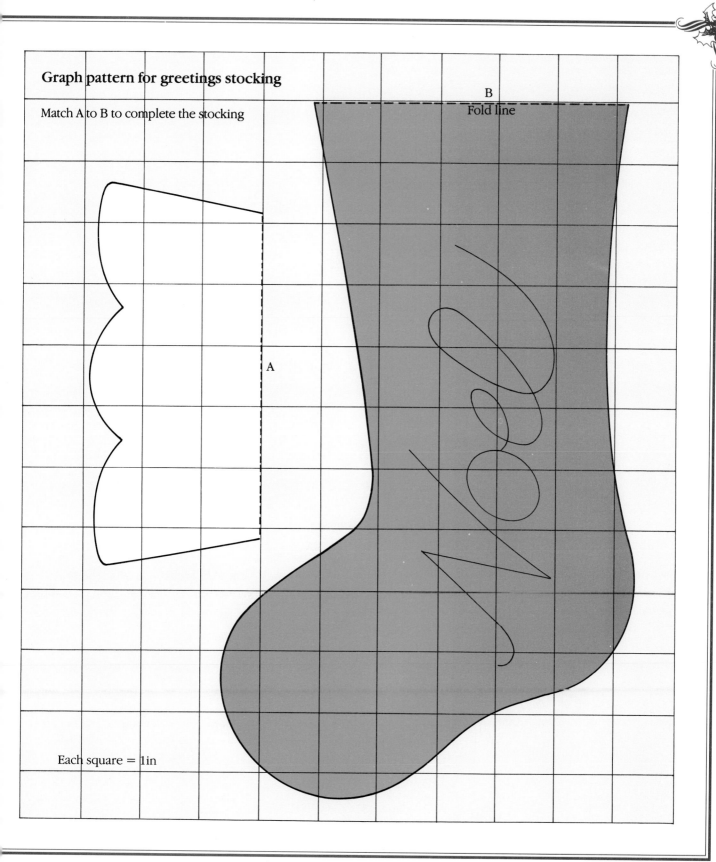

Graph pattern for greetings stocking

Match A to B to complete the stocking

B

Fold line

A

Noel

Each square = 1in

CHAPTER 5

The season for giving

Our grandmothers' Christmas catalogues were full of beautiful things to buy but they all knew that there was nothing quite so special as a handmade gift. The selection in this chapter includes knitwear for children, a charming apron with matching oven mitts for the Christmas cook and a variety of smaller gifts, such as decorated wooden spoons and a Christmas tree pillow worked in appliqué. Decorating with spices – a traditional Austrian folk art – and making iced gingersnap figures are just two of the crafts in this chapter that would make ideal pre-Christmas activities for the entire family.

Materials

½yd of 36in-wide white cotton fabric
8in square of red cotton fabric with
    white polkadots
6¾in square of green cotton fabric
12in square of lightweight polyester
    batting
Scrap of gold fabric (for star)
1⅜yd of 1¼in wide plain red binding (if
    you cannot find binding in the right
    color, buy red cotton fabric and join
    strips cut on the bias to make up the
    correct length)
1⅜yd of cording
1yd of ¼in-wide red ribbon
1yd of ⅜in-wide gold ribbon,
    edged with green
⅞yd of ¼in-wide green ribbon
Red, white, black, gold and green sewing
    thread
6 Christmas tree bells
12in-square pillow form
Tracing paper

Tree pillow

Light, bright and frivolous – this charming little appliqued pillow with its sewn-on bells and tiny ribbon bows can be added to scatter pillows on a chair or sofa to make an instant Christmas decoration. Its delightful impracticality and "just-for-today" air would make it an ideal gift to take as an extra for your hostess if you are visiting on Christmas day, and the perfect accompaniment to a more "sensible" present. The finished pillow cover measures approximately 11¼in square, with binding, and the appliquéd tree and star are stitched on, though they could just as well be sewn by hand, if you prefer.

Cutting out

From the white fabric, cut one piece measuring 12in square for the front and two pieces measuring 7¼in x 12in for the back of the cover. Check that the batting is the same size as the front cover piece and trim if necessary.

Trace the outlines of the tree, tub and star, given on page 127, drawing each shape separately so that there is no overlap, then cut them out from the tracing paper.

Use the tracing paper patterns to mark and cut out a tree from green fabric and tub from white fabric. Whether you intend to sew the appliqué by hand or with machine satin stitch, you should add an allowance of between ¼in and ⅜in all around each piece. The seam allowances are either turned under prior to hand sewing in place or trimmed away after machine stitching in position.

Gold fabric often ravels very easily, so do not cut out the star at this stage but mark the outline on the fabric with a pencil and then cut out around the shape, approximately ⅜in outside the points of the star. You may find that it helps if you iron the piece of gold fabric onto a scrap of fusible

interfacing to hold the threads securely and then cut out the shape.

Applying the motifs

Iron the pieces if necessary, then pin the tub and tree in position on the red square (turning under the seam allowance first if the shapes will be hand sewn in place). Baste each piece thoroughly, about ¼in in from the raw edge, then press the work again.

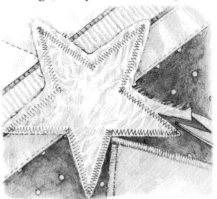

If you are machine stitching the appliqué, set your machine to a narrow satin stitch (close zigzag) and stitch the tree and tub in position along the marked outline, using matching green thread for the tree and white for the tub. Trim away the surplus fabric beyond the stitching using sharp embroidery scissors and cutting as closely as possible to the stitching line. Remove the basting thread.

If you are hand sewing the appliqué, sew around the turned-under edges with buttonhole stitch and then remove the basting thread.

Using green thread and a small straight stitch, make the decorative zigzag lines on the tub. Still using green thread and straight stitch, take the white front cover section and decorate it with diagonal lines of green stitching, set ¾in apart.

Using black thread, stitch in the trunk of the tree, either with short lines of machine straight stitch, set very close together, or with hand-sewn stitches.

Center the red appliquéd square over the front cover, with the wrong side of the appliqué facing the right side of the cover. Pin and baste thoroughly all around the edges. Cut the green ribbon into four 7⅜in strips. Tuck ¼in under at one end of each strip and lay the strips in a square, framing the appliqué design. Position the strips so that each finished edge covers the raw edge of another strip. Using green thread and straight stitch, sew the ribbon in position, sewing along each long side, close to the edge, and across the ends.

Cut the gold ribbon into four 8¼in strips and repeat the process, making sure that the gold ribbon butts up against the green.

Baste the star in position over the ribbon borders and sew it in place using gold thread and satin stitch.

Finishing the cover
Take the two pieces of white cotton fabric for the back of the cover and hem one long side of each: turn under ⅜in and press, then turn under another 1in and press again; using white thread and straight stitch, sew the fold in position, stitching close to the inner folded edge.

Lap the wrong side of one piece over the right side of the other, so that the first just covers the stitching line of the second. Stitching ⅜in in from the raw edges at either end of the hems, stitch across to hold the overlap in position. The joined pieces should now be the same size as the front cover.

Fold the red binding over the cording and, using red thread and the zipper foot of the sewing machine, stitch close to the cording so that it is enclosed in the binding. Next take the front cover and lay the batting on the wrong side of it. Pin and baste around the edges, then stitch the batting to the back of the cover, stitching just under ⅜in in from the raw edges. Lay the covered cord on the right side of the cover, with the raw edges of the casing

matching the raw edges of the cover. Pin and baste in position, clipping into the seam allowances of the casing at the corners as necessary.

Where the two ends meet (this should not be at a corner) they should overlap for about 1in. Undo the casing at each end and stitch the edges with a diagonal seam. Unravel the strands of the cord for the length of the overlap. Cut away two strands from one end and one strand from the other to reduce bulk. Twist the

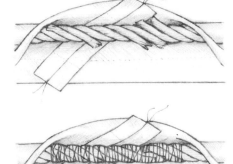

remaining strands together and bind them securely with thread. Do not pull the cord too tightly or the ends will work apart in wear. Fold the casing back over the cord.

Again using the zipper foot and red thread, stitch the covered cording to the front cover.

Lay the back cover over the front cover, with right sides together and stitch around the edge. Stitch as close to the cord as possible, to cover the previous row of stitching. Snip V-shapes into the seam allowances at the corners and turn the cover right side out.

Sew the bells in position, stitching through the front cover only. Cut the red ribbon into six equal lengths. Fold each strip into a bow shape, but do not knot them: sew them in position with red thread so that the thread forms the ribbons into bows and secures them to the front of the cover.

Measurement diagram for tree pillow

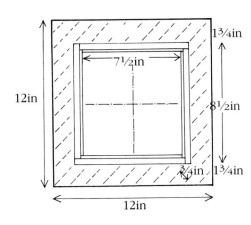

Trace pattern for tree pillow motifs

Materials

Chinese star anise
Cloves
Cinnamon (one stick)
Juniper berries
White peppercorns
Sprigs of dried butcher's-broom or other
 foliage (available from florists)
Silver stem wire
Tying wire
Brown stem binding tape
6 small pearl beads
1/4yd of fine gold cording
1/2yd of fine gold bullion
1/2yd of thick gold bullion
5/8yd of gold soutache or similar narrow
 braid trim
3/8yd of 1/8in-wide brown ribbon, edged
 with gold
Gold spray
10in x 6in piece of medium-weight
 brown cardboard
Tracing paper and pencil
X-acto knife
Clear glue
Hot glue

Spicy heart

This fragrant, spicy heart, decorated
with whole cloves, cinnamon, juniper
berries, star anise and peppercorns
bound with gold threads would make
a charming Christmas gift for a friend.
The making of these spice gifts is a
traditional Austrian folk art, originally
developed in Salzburg, and makes a
pleasant occupation for a cold winter's
day when there is little temptation to
go outside. The heart shown here
gives an idea of how the varied
elements of gold-wrapped cloves, star
anise and other spices can be used,
but give your imagination a free rein
and create your own decorations, gifts,
place settings and wreaths.

Cardboard base

First trace the heart shape and transfer
it to cardboard. Cut out one heart
shape, then use this as a template to
mark and cut out a second heart. Use
clear glue to stick the two shapes
together, brown side out, at the same
time inserting the gold cording,
formed into a loop, at the center top
of the heart.

Spray approximately 60 juniper
berries gold (you may need more if
yours are small) and set them aside to
dry. When they are dry, glue a row of
berries around the outside edge of the
heart, starting at the lowest point. Use
plenty of glue so that the berries are
firmly embedded in glue, and work in
short lengths to prevent the glue from
drying out before you have finished.

Next glue a row of natural juniper
berries inside the gold row. The inner
row is formed by alternating cloves
and white peppercorns: trim the stems
of the cloves as necessary, so that the
heads project beyond the inner edge
of the heart, the ends touch the inner
row of juniper berries and they
appear even in length.

Cover the outer edge of the
cardboard heart with gold soutache
braid, starting and finishing at the top
center of the heart.

Decoration

First take 15 well-shaped cloves and
prepare these. For each clove cut a
piece of thin bullion to go around the
head of the clove – approximately
5/8in to 7/8in long according to the size
of the clove. Cut a piece of stem wire
6in long and thread it through the
hollow bullion. Take one end of the
wire and thread it again through 1/8in
of bullion at the other end, then pull
the ends together to form a bullion
ring. Push this over the head of the
clove and wrap the ends of the wire
around the stem a few times. Cut a
short length of brown tape and wind it
around the stem and wire. When you
have prepared all 15 cloves, join them
into groups of five with tying wire and
again finish with tape.

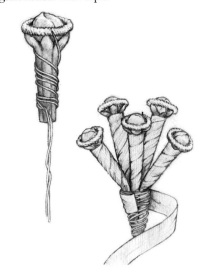

Break the cinnamon into two
unequal lengths and bind the pieces
together at one end. Cover the tying
wire with brown tape.

Cut off tips of butcher's-broom or
other foliage to make sprays about 2in
long. Tie them together in twos and
threes to make five small sprays.

Make two bullion spirals: cut the
thick bullion in half and thread silver
wire through each piece. For each
piece, let a short length of wire project
at one end and then bend this back
unobtrusively over the bullion, to

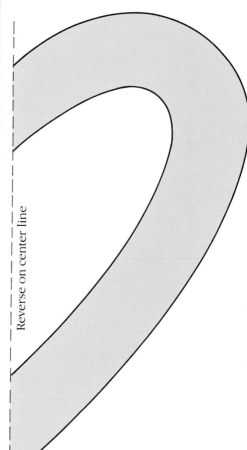

Trace pattern for heart

prevent it from slipping. Leave a longer length of wire at the other end and bind this with brown tape to make a stem. Coil the bullion around a knitting needle to form it into a spiral.

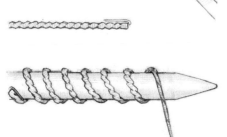

Next make a star anise flower (see far right). Start by breaking off any damaged pieces from the star and

gluing points into any gaps to make a full flower shape. Thread the six pearls on silver wire and twist it into a small circle. Thread a 2¼in length of fine bullion on silver wire and wind it around the pearl garland so that it twists between each pearl. Put the garland at the center of the star anise flower and twist the wire ends unobtrusively together at the back.

Assemble the various decorations at the top of the heart as shown in the picture, starting with the foliage sprays and gluing them firmly into position. Next glue the three bunches of cloves in place, then the bullion spirals and the cinnamon, and then the star anise flower. Finish by forming the ribbon into four loops, with 2¼in ends, and glue this in place to complete the heart.

Star anise

Christmas tree sweater

Here is a quick and simple way for a non-knitter to give a plain purchased sweater a festive air that is bound to delight the smaller branches of the family tree. The tree or other designs are embroidered onto the sweater using the technique demonstrated here, which is known as duplicate stitch. Originally a way of reinforcing threadbare woolens, it is now often used to decorate stockinette stitch knitwear by covering the stitches one by one, using lengths of colored yarn of an identical quality and thickness to that used in the knitting. For extra fun on Christmas day, you can add colored beads and star-shaped sequins to the trees – if they make the sweater look too specifically intended for Christmas they can always be taken off when the big tree is also stripped of its decorations. The tree motif is shown here on a sweater, but of course any piece of knitwear could be used as a base for your chosen motif, provided it is in stockinette stitch.

Duplicate stitch designs

The designs are worked by copying the chart. Each square on the chart represents one stitch on the knitted fabric. Since knitted stitches are rectangular rather than square, the design on the knitted fabric will appear more flattened than it does on the chart, so do not worry if your chart design seems to be slightly elongated and distorted.

The positioning of the motifs and the number of repetitions is up to you. You may find that it helps to make small paper cut-outs and pin these to the garment, moving them around until you have a satisfactory arrangement.

Use each color separately, working as much as possible from right to left and then from left to right, to keep the back of the work neat and smooth. Keep an even tension while stitching, taking particular care not to pull the

yarn too tightly. Finish off the ends at the back of the work by threading them through two or three stitches before cutting off the surplus yarn.

Working the design

1 Thread a blunt-ended wool needle with the chosen yarn and begin at the lower right-hand corner of the motif to be worked. Secure the end of the yarn at the back of the work by running it under several stitches. Bring the yarn through to the front through the base of the first stitch to be covered. Insert the needle from right to left behind the stitch above.

2 Pull the yarn through. Insert the needle through the base of the stitch and bring out through the base of the next stitch to the left.

3 Pull the yarn through, thus covering the first stitch. Continue in this way across the row, covering each stitch in turn and working from right to left.
4 Work the next row of stitches above the first, working from left to right, as shown below.

Materials

Purchased knitwear
Odds and ends of yarn in the same quality and thickness as the garment (if this is knitted in pure wool, and will not be washed too frequently, you may find that tapestry wools are an economical option)
Beads and sequins (optional – for tree decorations)
Blunt-ended wool needle

Chart for duplicate stitch tree motif

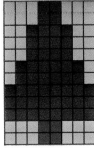

Each motif runs across 8 sts at its widest point and down 12 rows.

Materials

Knitting worsted weight yarn in amounts
and colors as foll:

Complete set
10½oz in red (A)
1¾oz in green (B)
1¾oz in white (C)
1 pair each of size 3 and 5 needles
Size C crochet hook (scarf only)
45 beads or small buttons for berries

Scarf
7oz in red (A)
1¾oz in green (B)
1¾oz in white (C)
18 beads

Hat
3½oz in red (A)
1¾oz in green (B)
1¾oz in white (C)
21 beads

Mittens
1¾oz in red (A)
1¾oz in green (B)
1¾oz in white (C)
6 beads

Gauge

24 sts and 32 rows to 4in on size 5
needles over st st.

Christmas knits

In bygone days, every member of the
household would be given a new
outfit at Christmas-time, and children
love to benefit from this tradition,
especially when the new clothes are as
bright and colorful as this delightful
set of scarf, hat and mittens. The scarf
measures approximately 9in by
45¼in and the hat and mittens are in
three sizes, to fit a 5[6:7] year old. All

are fairly quick and easy to knit. The abbreviations used in the pattern are given on page 113.

Scarf
Using smaller needles and A, cast on 54 sts. Work 8 rows in garter stitch (K every row).

Change to larger needles and beg with a K row, work 6 rows in st st.

Using a separate length of yarn for each leaf and twisting yarns when

changing colors to avoid holes, beg holly pat as foll:

1st row (K8A, K8B) 3 times, K6A.

2nd row P6A, (P8B, P8A) 3 times.

3rd row (K8A, K4B, K2A, K2B) 3 times, K6A.

4th row P6A, (P2B, P2A, P4B, K8A) 3 times.

These 4 rows set the holly pat. Cont working in this way from chart, beg with 5th row, until 14 rows have been completed. Break off B.

Work 6 rows in st st, using A only.

Using a separate length of yarn for each snowflake, beg snowflake pat as foll:

1st row K6A, *K2C, K8A, rep from * to last 8 sts, K2C, K6A.

2nd row P5A, *P4C, P6A, rep from * to last 9 sts, P4C, P5A.

3rd row K5A, *K4C, K6A, rep from * to last 9 sts, K4C, K5A.

4th row P6A, *P2C, P8A, rep from * to last 8 sts, P2C, P6A.

Beg with a K row, work 12 rows in st st, using A only.

17th row K1A, *K2C, K8A, rep from * to last 3 sts, K2C, K1A.

18th row P4C, *P6A, P4C, rep from * to end.

19th row K4C, *K6A, K4C, rep from * to end.

20th row P1A, *P2C, P8A, rep from * to last 3 sts, P2C, P1A.

Work 12 rows in st st, using A only.

These 32 rows form snowflake pat.

Rep snowflake pat until scarf measures approx 41¼in from beg, ending after 6 rows st st.

Work holly pat in reverse, turning chart upside down and beg with 14th row which is now first row as foll:

1st row K14A, K6C, (K10A, K6C) twice, K2A.

When chart is complete, work 6 rows in st st.

Change to smaller needles and work 8 rows garter stitch. Bind off.

Finishing the scarf

Using crochet hook and A, work a row of single crochet evenly along each long edge of scarf.

Cut sufficient 9in lengths of A ready to make a fringe at each end of scarf of approx 27 knots. Take 3 strands tog and, with RS facing, insert hook from back to front through main fabric at one end. Fold the 3 strands in half over hook, then pull looped yarn through fabric from front to back. Place hook around ends of yarn and draw ends through loop on hook. Pull strands tightly to make a neat knot. Rep along length of each end. Trim ends evenly.

Sew the berries in position as illustrated.

Hat

Using smaller needles and A, cast on 113(115:117) sts.

Work in K1, P1 ribbing for 3¼[3½:4]in, inc 1 st in last row. 114[116:118] sts.

Change to larger needles and work 6 rows in st st, beg with a K row.

Working colors as for scarf, beg working holly pat as foll:

1st row K1[2:3]A, *K6A, K8B, rep from * to last 1[2:3] sts, K1[2:3]A.

First row sets holly pat. Cont working from chart until 14 rows have been completed, keeping edge sts in st st and A. Break off B.

Work 6 rows in st st, using A only.

Working snowflake pat as for scarf, beg as foll:

1st row K7[8:9]A, *K1A, K2C, K9A, rep from *, ending last rep K8[9:10]A.

2nd row P7[8:9]A, P4C, *P8A, P4C, rep from * to last 7[8:9] sts, P7[8:9]A.

3rd row K7[8:9]A, K4C, *K8A, K4C, rep from * to last 7[8:9] sts, K7[8:9]A.

4th row P7(8:9)A, *P1A, P2C, P9A, rep from *, ending last rep P8[9:10]A.

Cont in st st in A only until hat measures 8½[9:9¾]in from beg, ending with a WS row.

Next row K0[2:1], *K3 tog, rep from * to end.

Thread yarn through rem sts, pull tightly and fasten off securely.

Finishing the hat

Sew the back hat seam. Make a pompon and sew to top of the hat. To make the pompon, cut two cardboard circles equal in diameter to the required size of the pompon (approx 3¼in). Cut smaller circles from the center of each. Using color A, wrap the yarn closely around both cardboard circles, placed together, passing it through the center and back over the outer edge each time, until the central hole is filled in.

With sharp scissors, cut through all the layers of yarn at the edges of the circles. Wrap a length of yarn several times around the center of the pompon, between the two circles, and knot tightly.

Cut away the cardboard and fluff out the pompon. If necessary, trim away any untidy ends, and use the tying ends to attach the pompon to the hat. Sew the berries in position as illustrated.

Right mitten

Using smaller needles and A, cast on 37[39:41] sts. Work in K1, P1, ribbing for 1½in, inc 1 st in last row. 38[40:42] sts. Change to larger needles and beg with a K row, work 2 rows in st st.

Shape thumb gusset

Working colors as for scarf, beg snowflake on palm as foll:
1st row K18[19:20]A, M1, K2A, M1, K8[9:9]A, K2C, K8[8:9].
2nd row P7[7:8]A, P4C, P29[31:32]A.
3rd row K18[19:20]A, M1, K4A, M1, K7[8:8]A, K4C, K7[7:8]A.
4th row P8[8:9]A, P2C, P32[34:35]A.
Working colors as for scarf, beg holly on back of hand as foll:
1st row K7A, K8B, K3[4:5]A, M1, K6A, M1, K18[19:20]A.
2nd row P29[31:33]A, P8B, K7A.
Last 2 rows set the holly pat, cont to work holly from chart on back of mitten, keeping palm in A only and inc as before until there are 52[54:56] sts.
Next row K1A, K2B, K2A, K6B, K23[24:25]A, turn.
Next row P16[16:18]A, turn.
Work across these sts for thumb.
Work 1¼[1½:1½]in in st st on these 16[16:16] sts, ending with a WS row.

Shape top of thumb

Next row K2 tog to end of row. 8[8:8] sts.
P one row.
Cut yarn, thread through rem sts, pull tightly and fasten off.
With RS facing rejoin yarn to base of thumb, pick up and K2 sts from base of thumb and K18[19:20 sts to end. 38[40:42] sts.
P one row, keeping holly pat correct. Beg working snowflake pat on palm as foll:
Next row K1A, K6B, K17[18:19]A, K2C, K12[13:14]A.
Next row P11[12:13]A, P4C, P16[17:18]A, P6B, P1A.
Next row K23[24:25]A, K4C, K11[12:13]A.
Next row P12[13:14]A, P2C, P24[25:26]A.
Work 12 rows in st st, using A only. Beg working snowflake pat as foll:
Next row K6[7:8]A, *K2C, K10A, rep from * once, K2C, K6[7:8]A.
Next row P5[6:7]A, *P4C, P8A, rep from * once, P4C, P5[6:7]A.
Next row K5[6:7]A, *K4C, K8A, rep from * once, K4C, K5[6:7]A.
Next row P6[7:8]A, *P2C, P10A, rep from * once, P2C, P6[7:8]A.
Using A only, cont in st st until mitten measures 2¾[3¼:3½]in from base of thumb, ending with a WS row.

Shape top of mitten

1st row *K1, K2 tog, K13[14:15], K2 tog tbl, K1, rep from * to end.
2nd and every other row P to end.
3rd row *K1, K2 tog, K11[12:13], K2 tog tbl, K1, rep from * to end.
5th row *K1, K2 tog, K9[10:11], K2 tog tbl, K1, rep from * to end.
7th row *K1, K2 tog, K7[8:9], K2 tog tbl, K1, rep from * to end
8th row P. Bind off.

Left mitten

Work as given for mitten, reversing position of pat.

Finishing the mittens

Sew thumb, top and side seams on each mitten. Sew berries in position.

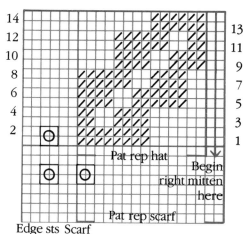

14
12
10
8
6
4
2

13
11
9
7
5
3
1

Pat rep hat
Begin right mitten here
Pat rep scarf
Edge sts Scarf

Key

A

B

Approx position for sewing on bead

Materials

Apron
3³⁄₈yd of 36in-wide plain, unbleached
    muslin
4³⁄₈yd of 5in-wide eyelet trim
1⁵⁄₈yd of 1in-wide ruffled eyelet trim
4in of touch-and-close tape such as Velcro
Matching sewing thread
Tailor's chalk or colored pencil
Tracing paper and long ruler

Oven mitts
¹⁄₂yd of 36in-wide cream quilted fabric
¹⁄₄yd of 36in-wide plain unbleached
    muslin
1¹⁄₄yd of cream bias binding
Matching sewing thread

Motifs
Tracing paper
Transfer pencil
Red and white fabric paints
Black permanent marker
Paintbrush

Cook's Christmas

Christmas can be a nerve-wracking time for the cook – at least until guests are eating and the compliments start coming in – so this pretty, old-fashioned calico apron, with its heart-shaped pockets and lacy trim, together with matching oven mitts, all cheerfully featuring Santa Claus himself, will be a welcome morale booster.

The set is so pretty and easily laundered that it could equally well be made without the Christmas motif, though the idea of having an apron reserved for the festive season has a charm of its own. On the practical side, it provides a perfect solution to the familiar problem of having to appear attractively dressed for a special occasion without risking damage to an expensive outfit.

Note Make sure when you buy the paints and the fabric that they are compatible: some transfer colors can only be used with synthetic fabrics and most fabric paints can only be used with natural fibers such as cotton. Check carefully and if you are not using muslin for the apron and oven mitts, make sure that you know the constituents of the fabric that you have chosen.

Cutting out

The first stage is to cut out the pattern pieces before transferring the design. For the apron, mark the pattern pieces on the fabric using a long ruler and either tailor's chalk or a colored pencil.

All the pattern pieces are cut out on the straight grain of the fabric. For the pockets, trace off the shape given on page 138, and cut out. When cutting out the fabric place the pattern on a fold as directed – it is easier to match the two sides of the heart if you cut out the pockets on the fold in this way. If you are also making the oven mitts, trace the oven mitt pattern given on pages 142-143.

For the apron, cut out the pattern pieces as follows:
Front – 36in wide x 31¹⁄₂in deep, cut one
Sides – 12¹⁄₂in wide x 31¹⁄₂in deep, cut two
Waistband – 23¹⁄₂in wide x 3in deep, cut two
Straps – 3in wide x 36in long, cut four
Tie ends – 6in wide x 36in long, cut two
Bib – 8in wide x 10¹⁄₄in deep, cut two
Pocket – heart shape, cut four

For the mitts, cut out three matching pairs from quilted fabric.

If the muslin to be used for the apron and the tops of the oven mitts has had any finishing chemical added to it, this might prevent the transfer design from coloring the fabric effectively, so wash the bib section and the non-quilted oven glove fabric and press them with a moderately hot iron. Mark the outlines of a matching pair of mitts on the plain muslin.

Transferring the design

Trace the design, using the transfer pencil. Do not trace the central registration mark with the transfer pencil, but copy this on the other side of the tracing, using an ordinary pencil.

Fold and press the bib section of the apron diagonally in half both ways and press, to find the center point. Lay the bib flat on your ironing board and either pin it or put strips of masking tape at the corners to hold it in position. Matching the central registration mark on the tracing with the pressed center of the bib, carefully place the design, transfer side down, over the fabric and, using a moderately hot iron, press until the outlines appear on the muslin.

For the oven mitts, you will need to make two separate tracings of the motif in order to reverse one motif to give a mirror image: make one tracing using the transfer pencil and for the second one trace the motif with an

Cutting layout

Front

Waistband

Side panels

Fold

Selvages

Strap

Strap

Strap

Strap

Tie end

Tie end

Bib | Pocket

Bib | Pocket

ordinary pencil and then turn it over and trace over the outlines on the back of the tracing, this time using the transfer pencil. Ignore the registration marks but carefully place the tracings over the fabric with the marked outlines, fitting them within the same space in each outline. Again using a

moderately hot iron, press until the outlines appear, making two matching Santas.

Go over the details on the bib and the mitts, this time using the black permanent marker. As when ironing, it will be easier if you tape or pin the fabric to your working surface.

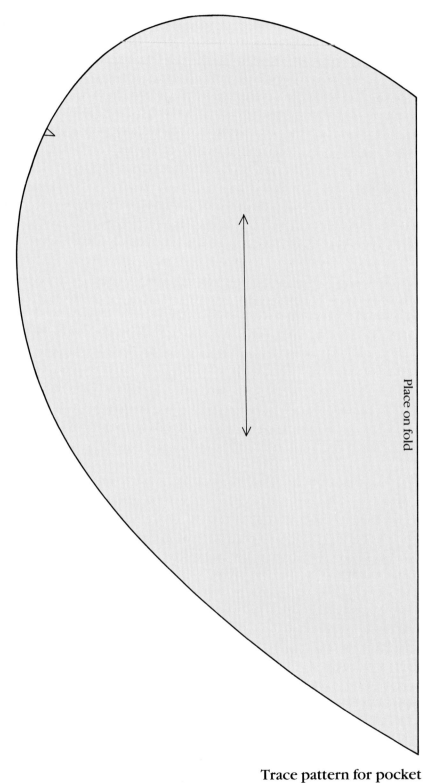

Place on fold

Trace pattern for pocket

Using the paintbrush, paint the red details on all three Santas, then paint the white details, taking care not to go over the marked lines.

Permanently fix the fabric paint to the fabric by ironing, following the manufacturer's instructions.

Alternative method

If, instead of using muslin or other natural fiber for the apron and oven mitt tops you have chosen a synthetic fabric, and if you are using transfer crayons instead of paints, the design is transferred by a slightly different process. Start by transferring the design to the fabric and going over the lines with the permanent marker, as already described.

When the outlines are on the fabric, take the tracings and, using red and white crayons, color in the details of the design on the three tracings. If the crayons do not work well on the tracing paper, you will have to copy the design onto poster board (again, three times, with one matching pair of heads) and color this. Take care not to leave any loose flakes of crayon on the colored drawings as these may mark the wrong part of the fabric. Cut the drawings out, cutting carefully around the outlines, again to avoid smudges.

Carefully place the colored drawings face down on the fabric and press, first making sure that your iron is not too hot for the fabric.

The apron
Preparing the skirt

With right sides together and making a ⅝in seam, stitch the side sections to the front panel. Press open and finish the edges.

At each side of the combined panel, turn ⅜in under along the raw edge and press, then turn under a further ⅝in and press, then straight stitch, close to the folded edge, to finish the sides.

Run two lines of gathering threads along the upper edge of the apron, starting 2in in from each end.

Pockets

Take one pocket piece (this now becomes a top pocket piece) and pin ruffled eyelet trim all around, matching the raw edge of the pocket with the raw, gathered edge of the trim, so that the lace lies on the right side of the pocket. Allow fullness around the curves. Pin and stitch the trim in position, with a scant ⅜in seam.

Place a second pocket piece (now pocket lining) on the first, with right sides together, and machine stitch around, leaving a 1½in opening at one side for turning and making a ⅜in seam. (Take care that the first stitching line will not show when the pocket is turned right side out.) Trim the seam and clip the curves, then turn the pocket right side out. Slip stitch the opening.

Repeat the process to prepare the second pocket. Pin the pockets to the skirt front with the outer notch 14¼in in from the side seam and 6½in down from the raw upper edge. Make sure the pockets are evenly positioned and then topstitch to secure, stitching around the lower edge, between the notches.

Bib

With right sides together stitch the painted bib front to the bib lining along the upper edge, with a ⅝in seam. Trim, turn and press the seam. Baste the lower edges together. Fold the bib to find the center of the lower edge and put a marker there.

Straps

The four strap pieces represent two top pieces and two lining pieces. Cut the remaining eyelet trim in half. Taper the ends of each strip as shown. Run a gathering thread along the raw edge of each strip.

Take one strap piece and pull up the gathers on a lace strip to fit the strap, starting and finishing 1¼in from the short edges. Pin and stitch the lace to the strap, with right sides

Trace pattern for Santa Claus motif

Center

together and raw edges matching. Press the seam toward the strap and trim the seam allowance to ¼in. Repeat for the other strap.

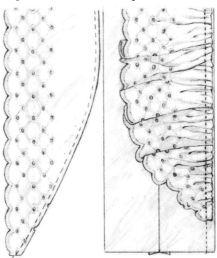

With right sides together and raw edges matching, pin and baste the straps to the outside edges of the bib.

On each strap lining, turn under a ⅝in allowance along one long edge and press, then trim the allowance to ¼in. Pin the strap linings (unpressed long edges) to the back of the bib, so the bib is sandwiched between the strap fronts and linings. Also pin the free ends of the straps and linings together, continuing on from the bib. Stitch the long edge of the straps, on the inside of the bib and across the short end. Trim the seam and cut across the corner. Press the seams flat and turn the strap pieces right side out, then pin and baste the folded edge of the linings to the fronts. Topstitch, working from the right side.

Finishing the apron

Pull up the skirt gathers to fit the waistband, starting and finishing ⅝in from either end of the band. Pin and stitch, then press the seam allowances toward the band.

At each side of the skirt and band, turn back the ungathered 2in to form an extended facing and press. Baste in position at the waistband.

Fold the skirt to find the center of the waistband and mark.

Take one of the tie pieces and make a ¼in double hem on both long sides. Fold the tie with right sides together and machine stitch making a ¼in seam, across one short end. Turn right side out, forming the end into a point, and press flat. Pleat the other end of

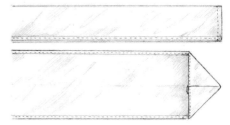

the tie to fit the depth of the waistband, with the finished edge of the tie ⅝in below the raw top edge of the waistband. Stitch tie to waistband.

Repeat for the second tie, and attach it in the same way.

With right sides and center fronts matching, pin and baste the bib to the waistband. On the remaining waistband facing, press one long (lower) edge ⅝in to the wrong side. Place the waistband facing wrong side up over the bib, matching the raw edge of the waistband. Pin and baste in position along the top edge of the waistband and the short sides, making sure that the ties lie inward, between the two bands. Stitch along the top edge and down both sides. Stitch across the ties and bib section a second time for added strength.

Trim seams and cut across the seam allowances at the corners, then turn right side out and slip stitch the folded edge of the waistband facing to the previous row of stitching.

Oven mitt

Cut out the decorated oven mitt fronts along the marked outline.

With wrong sides together, stitch one decorated front to one quilted mitt piece, making a ⅜in seam. Repeat for the other oven mitt, then

Trace pattern for oven mitt

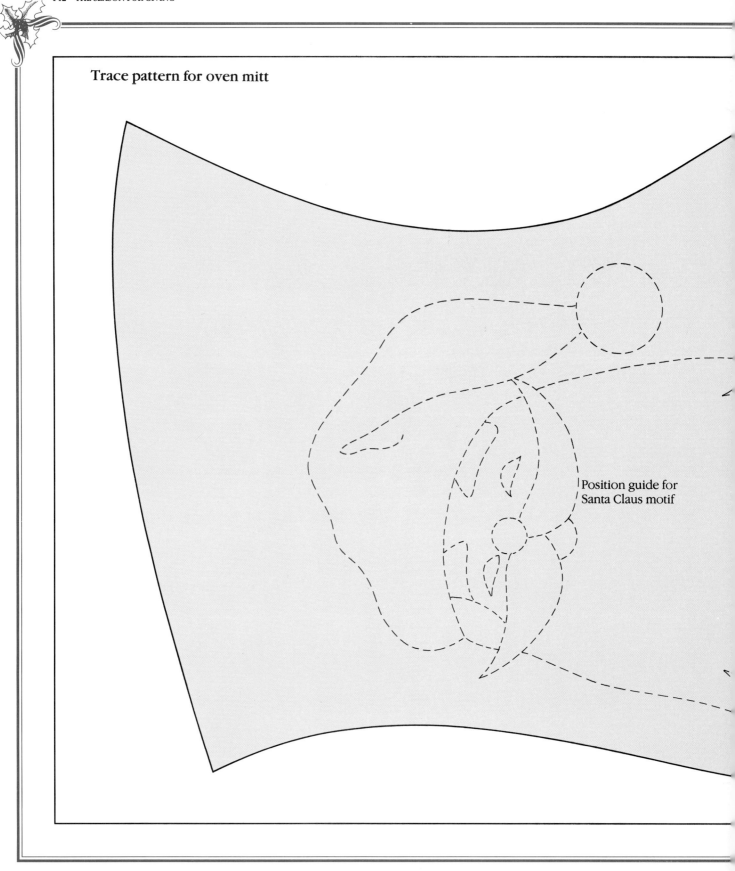

Position guide for
Santa Claus motif

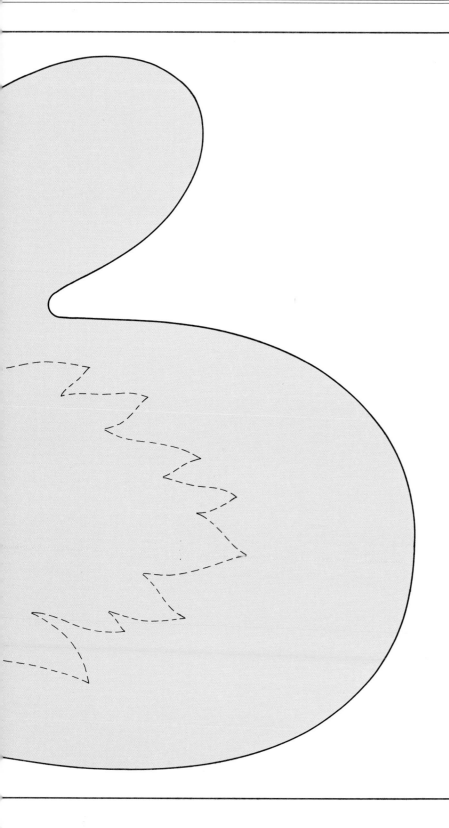

stitch the two pairs of quilted oven mitt pieces together, this time with wrong sides together.

At the seam allowances of the quilted fabric, undo the quilting to the seamline and trim back the batting as close to the stitching as possible, to remove excess bulk. Trim the seam allowances of the fabric and clip the curves at the thumb.

Turn decorated mitt sections right side out and insert a quilted mitt inside each one.

On each mitt, trim the inner lining at the wrist edge, to within ⅜in from the wrist edge of the outer mitt. Catchstitch in position at the seams and to the inside layer of fabric at the back of the outer mitt.

Machine stitch bias binding to the wrist edge of each mitt, stitching it to the right side with a ¼in seam. Fold the binding to the wrong side so that it is not visible on the right side, and slip stitch in place.

For each mitt, cut a 6¾in strip from the remaining binding and fold it in half lengthwise, with right sides together. Stitch close to the folded edges, then fold the strip into a loop and stitch it to the side seam of the mitt, on the inside.

Materials

One or more wooden spoons
Wood-burning tool
Fine sandpaper
Trace-down paper (available from art
    supply stores) – optional
Watercolors, poster paints or blendable
    color pencils
A firm, fine paintbrush
Varnish (an aerosol spray is the
    easiest to use)
⅜yd each of red, green and white
    ⅜in-wide satin ribbon

For the cook

These wooden spoons have been festively decorated using the technique of wood burning, a craft which has been practiced throughout the ages and throughout the world. The design outlines are lightly burned onto a wooden surface, producing a slightly raised appearance, which may be lesser or greater according to the degree of burning.

A simple wood-burning tool is not expensive to buy and can be obtained from crafts and hobby stores. If you do not want to try out this craft, you can obtain a similar effect by drawing the motifs on the spoons with a drawing pen. Note that the spoons are not recommended for cooking.

Wooden spoons are available in kitchen and hardware stores. It is best to choose spoons made of smooth wood of a light color and with an even grain, as these will show the motifs and colors to the best advantage.

Burning the design

Using a piece of fine sandpaper, thoroughly sand down the spoon, working in the direction of the grain until a smooth surface is obtained.

Either pencil in the motif of your choice, or make a tracing from the motifs given and copy it onto the back of the spoon with trace-down paper (any mistakes will be easier to erase than those made by ordinary carbon paper). Keep the lines clear and distinct, and make them as lightly as possible.

If a wood-burning tool is being used, always work on a heatproof surface and away from young children. Attach a medium to fine point (this is equivalent to the nib of a pen) and heat the point until it is just short of red hot. Test it on a scrap of wood to make sure that it does not burn too fast or too fiercely.

Any lines which are over-burned cannot be lessened, so it is best to work the design as lightly as possible, if necessary going over lines that are too faint a second time. Make the outline first, then the inner lines and details. Burn spots will appear if the point stops even for a second, so keep it moving. Once the wood burning is completed, lightly erase any remaining pencil marks with a clean, white eraser.

Alternative method

If the design is to be drawn with a pen instead of burned into the wood, the wood should be sealed after sanding with a sanding sealer solution, obtainable from hardware stores. This will prevent the ink from bleeding into the grain of the wood.

Experiment on a spare piece of wood to make sure that your pen is suitable before drawing the outline on the spoon.

Coloring and finishing

To color in the motifs, use sharpened, blendable color pencils, or apply watercolors or poster paints with a small, firm paintbrush within the marked outlines.

Allow the decorations to dry thoroughly, preferably overnight, and then give the spoon several light coats of spray varnish until you have obtained a suitable finish.

Complete each spoon with a satin bow, tied around the handle.

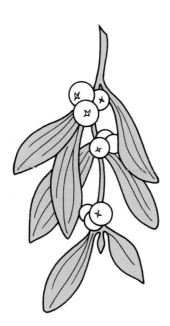
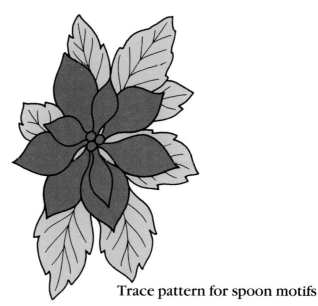

Trace pattern for spoon motifs

Quantities

This is enough for two Santas (complete with sleigh) and six kings.

2½ cups sifted all-purpose flour
½ cup margarine
⅓ cup light molasses
3½ tablespoons sugar
3 teaspoons fresh root ginger (grated on the fine side of a cheese grater)
1 teaspoon baking soda
1 teaspoon ground cinnamon
1 egg, well beaten

Decoration

1¾ cups confectioners' sugar
Gumdrops
Dragées (in mixed colors)
Chocolate sprinkles
Nonpareils
Green, red, blue and yellow food coloring

Templates

Tracing paper
Medium-weight cardboard
Spray glue
X-acto knife

Gingersnap figures

These gingersnap kings and Santa Claus (pulling his own sleigh to give the reindeer a rest) are so decorative that it will be hard to start eating them, and so delicious that it will be hard to stop once you break through your inhibitions. Children will love helping to make them and adding the finishing touches. In fact if you are giving a small children's party it would be fun to prepare the dough and the templates beforehand, make the cookies together at the party, and let each child take one home as a gift.

Making templates

First trace the outlines of the kings and Santa Claus. Cut out the shapes, leaving a margin of about ⅜in around each one.

Using spray glue, attach the tracing paper outlines to cardboard, then cut out, following the outlines accurately.

Making the cookies

Measure the light molasses into a cup and stand it in a pan of hot water to warm, or microwave it for a few seconds.

Heat the oven to 300° and grease two baking sheets.

Cream the margarine and sugar and then add the dry ingredients, the well-beaten egg and the molasses. Mix until you have a stiff dough. Knead the dough very thoroughly.

Roll the dough out on a floured board until it is about ⅜in thick. Place the templates in position. Using either a very sharp kitchen knife or the X-acto knife, cut around the outlines.

Carefully smooth any rough edges with your fingers then, using a spatula, gently lift the shapes and arrange them on the baking sheets. Make sure that you allow plenty of space around each cookie.

Bake for one hour (for softer cookies, bake for 10 to 15 minutes at 350°, though these may not hold their shape quite so well).

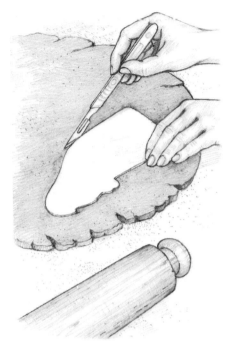

After baking, place the cookies on a wire rack to cool.

Decorating the cookies

Sift the confectioners' sugar into a bowl and then beat in enough water to give a thick consistency that is suitable for piping.

Divide the icing into five cups and add drops of food coloring, mixing it in until you have one cup with the original white icing, one cup with red, one with green, one blue and one with yellow (add a very small amount of red if necessary, to achieve a gold color). You will only need a small amount of the gold, and more red and white than blue and green.

Using a wide nozzle, pipe the icing onto the cookies. Cover all the areas in any one color and allow it to dry before changing to the next.

When you have finished icing, add the decorations as indicated on the diagrams. They must all be added as soon as you have finished icing, before the icing has hardened.

The cookies can be stored for up to three weeks in an airtight can.

Trace patterns for gingersnap figures

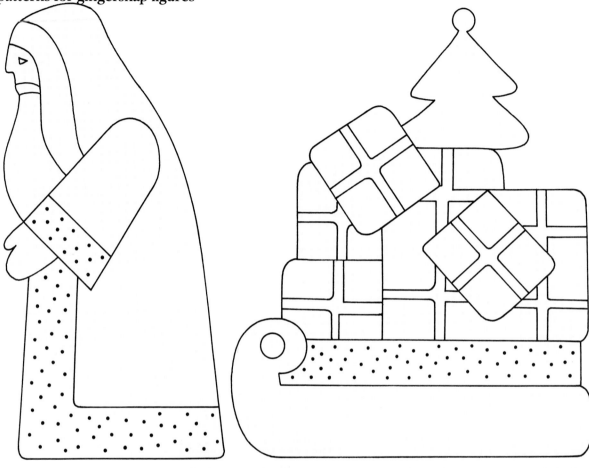

Santa Claus and sleigh

Three kings

CHAPTER 6

The Christmas table

Every skilled hostess knows that it is not just excellent and beautifully presented food, but those all-important finishing touches that create a certain atmosphere and turn a delicious meal into a special and memorable occasion. The right lighting, such as a set of the angel candle holders featured here, an attractive centerpiece, special place mats and napkins, made just for the day, and perhaps napkin rings like the jolly Santa Claus shown on page 158 – they are all part of the Christmas scene, and help to transform a familiar room into a magical setting that will stay in the mind of every child present for a lifetime.

Materials

2¼yd of 36in-wide heavy white cotton
    drill or similar fabric (this is enough
    for six mats and a runner for a 6ft-
    long table)
Sewing thread in green (for the zigzag
    outlining)
Anchor stranded embroidery floss:
    one skein of red #305 (for the berries)
Dressmaker's carbon paper
Tracing paper
Paper (11¾in x 16½in for making
    pattern – see directions)
Ruler and pencil
Sharp embroidery scissors
Embroidery hoop, 8in across (optional)

Holly place mats

A beautiful table setting, with
embroidered place mats and runner,
creates a festive atmosphere,
emphasizing that this is a special
occasion. The place mats shown here
are embroidered largely by machine
so they are relatively quick to make,
and though you may use them for
Christmas parties and for the twelve
days of Christmas itself, they can be
taken out each year to mark the start
of the season. The place mats in our
photograph are plain white, but the
background could equally well be
pale green or yellow if either of those
would go with your china.

Making the pattern

For the place mat, first trace the semi-
circle, given on page 154, tracing the
outline in parallel lines, as shown, and
reversing it on the center line, to
complete the oval mat. On the same
tracing, trace the holly motif in a
similar way, positioning it at one
corner, as indicated by the dashed
lines.

The pattern for the runner is made
in a similar way, with a straight strip of
paper 10¼in wide and a semi-circle at
each end. An overall length of 40in
would be appropriate for a 6ft table,
assuming that there would be a place
setting at each end of the table, but the

best way to be sure that you have got
the length of the runner right is to
measure your own dining table before
making the pattern.

Or you may prefer a longer runner
(allowing the ends to fall over the
edges of the table), with place settings
along each long side.

Embroidery

Using dressmaker's carbon paper,
transfer the outlines of the place mats
and the runner onto the fabric, using
the paper patterns and positioning the
shapes as shown in the cutting layout.
Remember that the holly motif
projects beyond the oval outline and
that you need to allow extra space
between mats.

Using a close zigzag, stitch around
the edges of the place mats and the
outlines of the holly leaves. Cutting
the place mats apart first makes it
easier, but leave a margin of fabric at
least 1¼in wide around each mat,
including the motifs. If you cut too
close to the outline, it is more difficult
to stitch.

Some people find it easier to work
machine satin stitch (close zigzag) if
the fabric is held in an embroidery
hoop. In this case, do not cut out the
mats, but put the fabric in a small
hoop so that the holly motif is in the
center of the ring and the fabric can
lie flat on the machine, marked side

Cutting layout

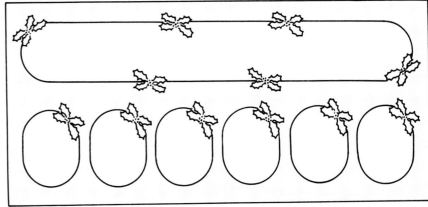

Place on fold

Trace pattern for place mat

Position guide for holly motif

up. This will prevent your having to hold the fabric taut as you stitch the details of the motifs. The outlines of the mats can more easily be stitched without a hoop.

The berries are hand embroidered in straight satin stitch, using three strands of embroidery floss. To work the satin stitch, bring the needle up on one edge of the berry, carry the thread across to the opposite edge and return under the fabric close to the starting point. Work the next stitch close to the first, making sure that no background fabric shows in between. For a raised effect, work over the stitches a second

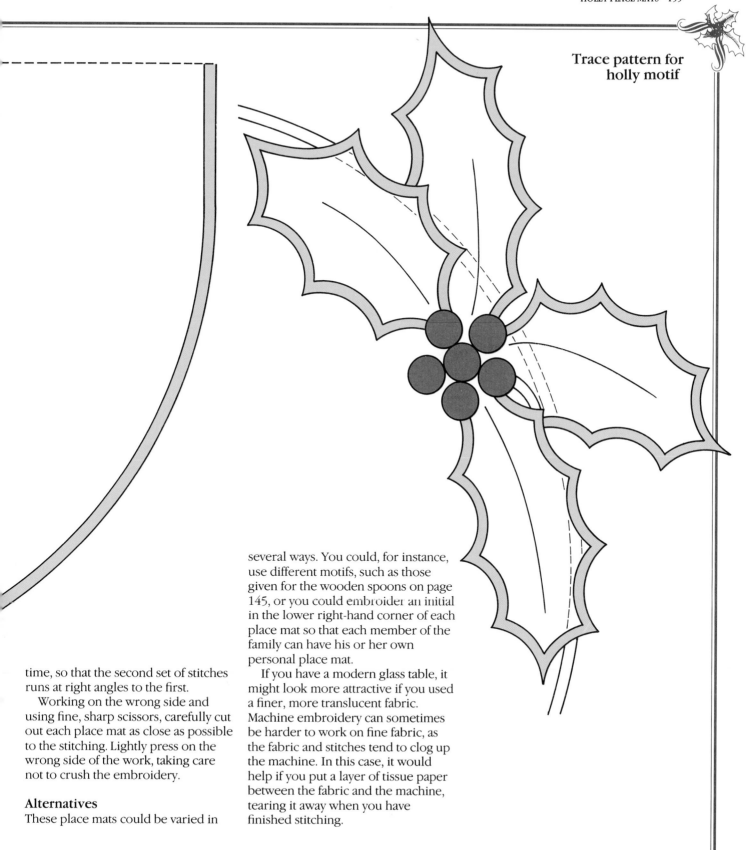

Trace pattern for holly motif

several ways. You could, for instance, use different motifs, such as those given for the wooden spoons on page 145, or you could embroider an initial in the lower right-hand corner of each place mat so that each member of the family can have his or her own personal place mat.

If you have a modern glass table, it might look more attractive if you used a finer, more translucent fabric. Machine embroidery can sometimes be harder to work on fine fabric, as the fabric and stitches tend to clog up the machine. In this case, it would help if you put a layer of tissue paper between the fabric and the machine, tearing it away when you have finished stitching.

time, so that the second set of stitches runs at right angles to the first.

Working on the wrong side and using fine, sharp scissors, carefully cut out each place mat as close as possible to the stitching. Lightly press on the wrong side of the work, taking care not to crush the embroidery.

Alternatives
These place mats could be varied in

Materials

Red napkin
Two small jingle bells
1³⁄₈yd of ¹⁄₈in-wide emerald green ribbon
Fabric glue
Short length of fine wire
White napkin
27 large green leaf sequins
Eight ¹⁄₈in-diameter red plastic beads
Three ¹⁄₄in-diameter red plastic beads
White sewing thread
Green napkin
Scraps of lace trim
Fusible web or fabric glue

Christmas napkins

Small finishing touches like these decorated napkins, with their added trims, make all the difference to a Christmas table setting. Purchased napkins have been used here, but you could easily make your own by hemming 16in squares of an appropriate fabric.

Red napkin

Cut two pieces of ribbon 8in long and two pieces each 4¹⁄₂in long. Thread an 8in length into a long-eyed needle. Leaving an end about ³⁄₄in long on the underside of the napkin, sew up to a corner, starting 6¹⁄₈in from the corner and ⁵⁄₈in from the edge. Sew a line of long running stitches parallel to the edge, about ³⁄₈in in length, and stop ⁵⁄₈in from the adjoining edge at the corner. Secure the other end to the underside with a dot of fabric glue and leave a tail of ribbon at the corner.

Thread the other 8in length of ribbon and sew a line of running stitches ⁵⁄₈in from the adjoining edge, up to the same corner, so that the second line is at right angles to the first. Where the two ends of ribbon meet, at the corner, tie them into a neat knot, then thread a jingle bell on each tail and knot them on. Glue the other end of the second length of ribbon in place as for the first.

Using fabric glue, glue the two 4¹⁄₂in strips to the napkin to meet in a corner, keeping parallel to the first two pieces and 1¹⁄₄in in from the edge of the napkin.

Set aside a 3in piece of the remaining length of ribbon and wind the rest around a 2in-wide piece of cardboard. Slide the ribbon off the cardboard and secure the loops together at the center by wrapping the fine wire around them. Push the ends of the wire through the knots securing the jingle bells. Use the remaining piece of ribbon to cover the wire and leave two ends coming down between the bells. Spread out the four ribbon ends which now hang down from the bells so that two ends lie to one side of the corner and two to the other. Use small dots of glue to secure the ends in place.

White napkin

Measure 1in up from the edge of the napkin and 4¹⁄₂in from the edge at one corner. Place the tip of a leaf sequin at this point and sew it in position. Attach a small red bead to the base of the leaf then sew two more leaves at an angle to the first, with their bases approximately ¹⁄₄in from that of the first, making a small cluster.

Make three more clusters in the same way, always working toward the corner and keeping parallel to the edge of the napkin.

Measure away from the corner again and repeat the process on the other side of the corner, making four more clusters. Fill the space that remains at the corner with the last three sequins and the three larger beads.

Green napkin

At one corner of the napkin, make a pattern with the lace motifs, cutting them apart first if necessary. When you are happy with the arrangement, fuse the motifs to the napkin using the fusible web.

Santa Claus napkin rings

A delightful piece of fun to complete your table setting, these frivolous napkin rings are very quick to make and guarantee that your Christmas dinner will start with laughter. The ring itself is just the hair, face and beard: the body is formed from the folded napkin. The quantities given below are sufficient for one ring only, but when you are making rings ready for the day, make a few more than the anticipated number of your guests in case there are any last-minute additions to the party (or in case you want to give any to your guests to take home with them).

Method
Trace off the outline and make a cardboard template (see page 50). Use the template to draw the outline on the back of the fur fabric, making sure that the fur will run down from the top of the finished ring. Cut out the shape. Then mark and cut out the central face shape; this must be carefully cut in one piece and kept, to be used for the whiskers.

Glue the felt rectangle to the wrong side over the cut-out face area. Brush the fur carefully in position around the face and trim it above the face. Glue the eyes in position.

Fold the cut-out fur section in half lengthwise and glue the wrong sides together. Form the strands into whiskers and glue the additional whiskers to the bottom of the face. Attach the berries to the holly and glue the decoration in position to one side of the face.

Trim away the fur for ⅝in at one end of the piece and glue the other end over this to form a ring.

Materials
Approximately 8in x 4in piece of white fur fabric with a long, silky pile
1½in x 1¾in piece of flesh-colored felt
Two ¼in-diameter eyes with movable centers
Small, three-leaf paper holly triangle
Two red berries
Fabric glue
Red table napkin
Tracing paper and lightweight cardboard

Trace pattern for beard

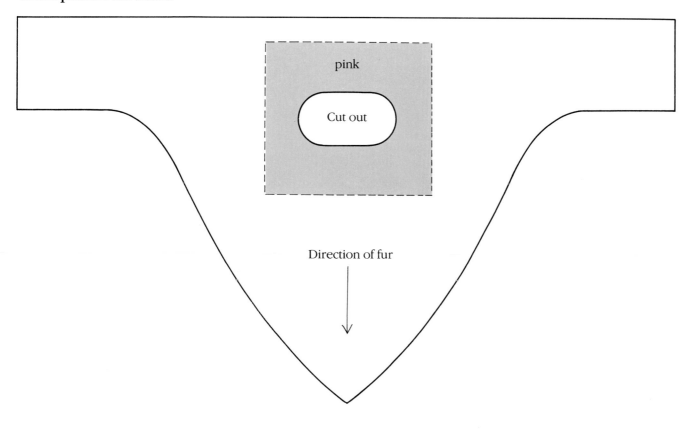

pink

Cut out

Direction of fur

Materials

10in plastic ring filled with water-
   absorbent foam such as Oasis (available
   from florists)
Sprigs of cypress, pine, holly and ivy
20 small pine cones
30 holly berries (available from florists
   – if your holly has no berries)
Gold spray
1⅜yd of ·1in-wide red ribbon
Floral wire, #18 gauge
Four medium-sized red candles

Evergreen centerpiece

Candlelight adds softness and a glowing luster to a Christmas table set with gleaming silver and crystal, creating the right ambience for a memorable occasion. This evergreen circle, set with four candles, is very quick and easy to make and can be prepared in advance (though not so far ahead that the greenery doesn't look fresh on the day). Take care that you do not leave the room unattended while the candles are lit, in case they burn too far down. Any drips of wax should be caught in the greenery, but you might want to put a mat or a circle of aluminum foil underneath.

Preparation

Spray the pine cones and let them dry on a sheet of newspaper before wiring them with 8in lengths of floral wire (see page 12).

Gather the holly berries into bunches of twos and threes and bind them together with lengths of floral wire.

Cut the ribbon into four equal lengths and tie each length into a bow. Thread a length of floral wire through the back of the knot of each bow.

Thoroughly soak the Oasis until it has absorbed as much water as possible.

Making the centerpiece

Work on a flat surface, turning the ring around as you work and constantly checking to make sure that you have an even distribution. It will help if you first arrange the greenery into bunches, according to type.

Start at the outer edge of the circle, alternating sprigs of cypress and holly and pushing them firmly into the ring. Make sure that the circle does not become misshapen.

At the top of the ring, push in the ivy, pine cones, berries and ribbons, arranging the cones in circles where you intend to position the candles. Fill the inner edge of the circle with small sprigs of pine.

Finish by pushing the candles firmly into the ring. Incidentally, if you are unfortunate enough to end up with a few drops of candle wax on your tablecloth, the best way to remove them is by pressing the cloth between layers of paper towels, using a reasonably hot iron.

Angel candle holder

Made from wood and decorated with acrylic paints, this little angel is designed to shed gentle candlelight on your Christmas festivities. The wood quantities given are sufficient for just one angel, which would look charming as a centerpiece inside a table decoration. If you are feeling ambitious, you could make several, to face out from the center of the table. The design is carefully contrived so that the wings counterbalance the front portion, which holds a small size Christmas candle. Do not use long candles or you will spoil the look of the design and, more importantly, make it unstable.

Cutting the pieces

You do not need a special workbench for this simple piece, but when cutting the wood always fix it to the table edge with a clamp. Protect the table and the wood surface with either folded up newspaper or flat wood scraps. Do not attempt to cut wood that is not clamped down.

For best results, use good quality acrylic paint and matte varnish. In the same way, check the wood carefully before you buy it and reject any pieces that have knots or may have been split. If you do have to use wood with knots, seal these with knothole sealer before painting.

First trace the pattern for the body and transfer it to the ¾in-thick wood. It is essential to make absolutely sure that the line at the base of the foot is straight, as the overall balance of the candle holder depends on this. Hold the marked wood in place on the table with a strong clamp and then cut the base line and any other reasonably straight lines with a hack saw. Use a fret saw for the finer curves.

Cut the ⅜in-thick wood in half and bind the two pieces firmly together with masking tape. Trace the wing and arm patterns and transfer these to the wood following the straight grain.

Using a combination of hack saw and fret saw as before, cut through the doubled wood to cut a pair of wings and a pair of arms. Once again, make sure before you start that the wood is fixed to the table top with a strong clamp.

Trace and transfer the flower-shaped candle base to a remaining piece of the ⅜in-thick wood. A hole will be drilled at the center of the shape for the candle, so before you start, fix the wood to the table with a clamp, placing a scrap piece of wood underneath the area which is to be drilled. This will help to prevent the wood from splitting.

Using the brace and bit, drill a hole in the center of the flower shape, drilling right through the wood, then carefully cut around the flower outline with a fret saw.

Mark out the rectangular shape, which is combined with the flower to make the holder, on a scrap of ¾in-thick wood. Cut it out carefully, making sure that you have a perfect cube, with the cut sides absolutely at right angles to the top and bottom. In the finished holder, the cube is turned on edge and the candle is held in one long (cut) side edge of this cube.

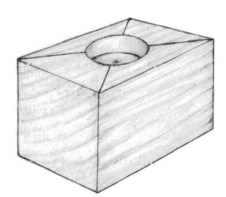

When you have cut the cube, therefore, turn it so that this side faces up. Lightly pencil in diagonal lines from corner to corner across this side to find the center point, then drill the center to a depth of ¼in, using the same bit as before.

Materials

9in x 4in piece of ¾in-thick fir or pine (planed and ready for use)
20in x 4in piece of ⅜in-thick fir or pine (planed and ready for use)
One 1¼in panel pin
Woodworking glue
White and gold acrylic paint
Matte varnish
One large and one fine sable brush for painting the details in acrylic paint
Brush for varnish

Tools

Hack saw
Fret saw
Brace and ⅝in drill bit
Clamps
Medium and fine sandpaper
Flat and curved sanding blocks

Mark the center of the base of the cube and gently tap the panel pin into place. This sticks into the base of the candle to hold it secure.

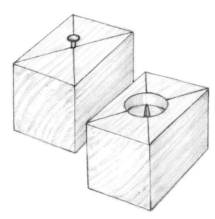

Sand the cube and the candle base, sanding the rims as well as the surfaces and using a combination of the flat and rounded sanding blocks. Start with the medium sandpaper and finish with the fine. Where possible, sand along the grain of the wood.

Sand the arms and the wings in the same way, making sure that the palms of the hands are flat. Sand the body of the angel, checking carefully that the feet are level.

Painting and assembly

Using the larger sable brush and white paint, paint the cube and the dress, covering both sides of the body and stopping at the neck. Paint the arms white to the wrist, leaving the hand and the inside surface of each arm unpainted. Leave them to dry.

Paint the hair, wings and feet and the side and top edges of the flower-shaped candle base with gold paint. Leave them to dry.

When the body is completely dry, use the fine brush and the gold paint to make the decorative lines and dots of gold on the dress. If necessary, paint these details twice.

The final stage is to glue the pieces together. Use a good quality woodworking glue and at each stage allow the glue to dry thoroughly

before moving on to the next. Start by gluing the flower-shaped candle base to the cube, matching up the drill holes. Leave it to dry.

Next glue the hands to the cube: place the hands parallel to and just under the bottom of the candle base. Use a scrap piece of ¾in-thick wood as a spacer at the shoulder end to keep the arms a parallel distance apart. When the hands are firmly

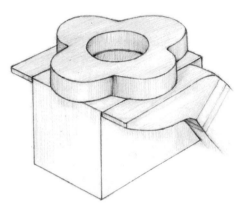

attached to the holder and the glue has dried, glue the arms to the body, following the lines marked on the pattern.

The position of the wings is crucial to the balance of the body, so mark the gluing line carefully on each side of the body. Double-check by attaching the wings to the body with masking tape and mark the correct position carefully.

Glue the wings to the body. As with the arms, use a scrap piece of ¾in-thick wood as a spacer to hold the wings absolutely parallel to each other while the glue dries.

Leave the assembled angel for 12 hours and then give it a coating of matte varnish. Leave it to dry and then apply a second coat.

Warning

As the candle holder is made of wood it will ignite if the candle is left to burn away, so never leave it unattended!

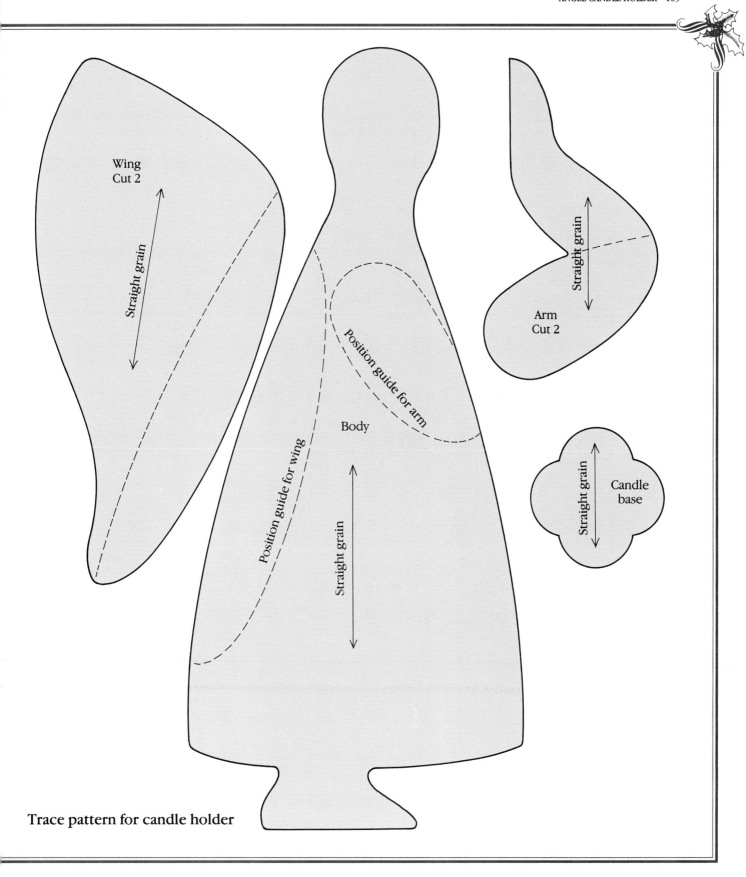

Wing
Cut 2

Straight grain

Position guide for arm

Body

Position guide for wing

Straight grain

Arm
Cut 2

Straight grain

Straight grain

Candle
base

Trace pattern for candle holder

Index

Acknowledgments

Project contributors
Jeanette Appleton: page 80
Gisella Banbury: pages 42, 124
Shiels Coulson: page 152
Alan Dart: page 113
Caroline Dewing: pages 32, 118
Julia Dumbrell: page 132
Valerie Green: page 115
David Hawcock: pages 27, 36, 39, 67, 74, 77, 95
Christina Korth: pages 12, 23, 160
Shelley Lazar: page 84
Fiona Neville: page 163
Bonnie Phipps: pages 50, 91, 146
Fiona Ryan: pages 21, 144
Pamela Westland: pages 15, 16, 18
Gloria Wittke: pages 44, 47, 54, 58, 88, 128, 136, 156, 159

Illustrators
Denis Hawkins: page 131(br)
Sally Holmes: pages 12, 15, 20, 22, 25, 26, 28, 32, 34, 37, 39, 41, 43, 44, 77, 92(t), 116, 120, 126, 128, 129(b), 140, 146, 156, 163, 164
John Hutchinson: pages 23, 28(t), 29, 35, 36, 40, 42, 46, 49, 52/3, 54, 55/6, 61, 62/3, 68/9, 70/1, 72/3, 74, 78/9, 82/3, 86, 88/9, 92(b), 93, 98/9, 100/1, 102/3, 117, 118, 121, 126(bl), 127, 129(t), 135, 137, 138/9, 142, 145, 148/9, 152, 154/5, 159, 165
Coral Mula: page 131(c)

Photographers
Simon Butcher: pages 106, 108, 110, 111, 112
Christmas Archives & Photo Library: pages 7, 8, 10, 16, 30, 33, 41, 64, 89, 104, 122, 143, 148, 150, 160
Ray Duns: pages 13(r), 14, 15, 17, 18/19, 21, 27, 32/3, 37, 38, 45, 48, 51, 55, 58/9, 60, 66, 75, 76, 81, 96, 116, 119, 125, 132/3, 137, 147, 161
John Melville: page 13(1)
Brian Nash: page 107
Peter Reilley: pages 24, 42, 85, 87, 90, 102, 129, 141, 144, 153, 157, 158, 162

For information on how you can have *Better Homes & Gardens*
magazine delivered to your door, write to:
Robert Austin, P.O. Box 4536, Des Moines, IA 50336.